From the Beginning

Resources and Study Guide to the Middle East

Betty Jane Bailey

FRIENDSHIP PRESS • NEW YORK

We are grateful to several publishers and authors for permission to reprint excerpts from their publications. These permissions are cited where the excerpts appear.

ISBN 0-377-00241-0
Editorial Office: 475 Riverside Drive, Room 860, New York, NY 10115
Distribution Office: P.O. Box 37844, Cincinnati, OH 45222-0844
Copyright © 1992 by Friendship Press, Inc.
Manufactured in the United States of America

Library of Congress Cataloging-in-Publication Data

Bailey, Betty Jane.
    From the beginning : resources and study guide to the Middle
East by Betty Jane Bailey.
        64 p.   cm.
    Includes bibliographical references.
    ISBN 0-377-00241-0 : $6.95
    1. Middle East—Study and teaching. 2. Middle East—Religion—
Study and teaching. I. Title.
DS61.8.B35 1992
956—dc20   91-39528
                                                                                CIP

Contents

To Susan and Omar,
who committed themselves at their wedding
"to bring aspects of the Middle East to their home
here and to bring aspects of the United States to their
home in the Middle East."

Introduction

Visions of St. Paul went through our heads as we hunted for the building on the Street called Straight in the old city of Damascus, Syria. We were received in a modest and modern office on the second floor of an ancient building, cool and dim after the hot, dusty streets. He was a charming man, quiet spoken and with hands that moved with grace and dignity. He answered our questions with thought and broad, friendly smiles, admitting that he was, indeed, the product of the youth movement among the Orthodox and that he believed in youth as the future of the church.

We addressed him as "Your Beatitude" and it seemed quite natural to do so even though we were Protestants through and through. The man was Ignatios IV, with the title of Patriarch of Antioch and All the East. We asked him if he wasn't impatient to see the fruits of the ecumenical movement in this area and what the future for today's youth would be. He chuckled about modern impatience and then he said to us, "Remember, Christianity is not a Western religion. My church was founded by Paul and Barnabas in the city of Antioch. We are the continuous incarnation of Christ in the area."

If we were to ask why Education for Mission/Friendship Press chose the Middle East as a current ecumenical study theme, the prominence of the area in the newspapers and the long years of concern for peace are certainly answer enough. But a more important answer is embodied in the story above. The Middle East is the birthplace of Christianity, and many of the churches there can claim a continuous presence from the beginning of Christianity. Even today these Christians are witnessing to their faith in very trying circumstances. Christians, such as those in the group you will be leading, will find it essential to learn about this work and witness as a way of developing a clearer understanding of Christian commitment to the work of reconciliation and peace in this area of the world.

This study guide is only one of several pieces published by Friendship Press concerning the Middle East. Its goal is to help you and your group study the theme together, utilizing a variety of resources. It adds its own "angle of vision" to the resources with an emphasis on learning about Middle Eastern cultures, particularly those of the Arabs, and its stories of indigenous (local) people. Other resources include *Angle of Vision: Christians and the Middle East* by Charles Kimball; "Map 'n' Facts: The Middle East"; and the videos "Celebration of Life" and "After the Storm." See the inside back cover for a complete description of these Friendship Press resources.

The course, included here, is made up of six study sessions of one to one and one-half hours. Suggestions for extending or condensing the course are included after Session Six. See Additional Learning Experiences, page 27. Beginning on page 29 there is a Resource Section containing material you will need in the study sessions, general cultural materials and a bibliography, filmography, and helpful addresses. The first part of the Resource Section contains worship ideas, profiles of Middle Easterners, charts and maps. The cultural materials are drawn from such areas as folktales and proverbs; recipes and information about food; names in Arab cultures; and phrases in some Middle Eastern languages.

Preparation for the leader

Begin your preparation several weeks before the course begins. Include tasks in these areas:

1. Publicize the course and encourage people to sign up. The conflicts in the region and media focus on the Middle East should generate a basic interest in the course. Emphasize the role of the churches and the particular approach you will be taking.

2. Order resources from Friendship Press. A copy of *Angle of Vision: Christians and the Middle East* by Charles Kimball should be made available to each participant. A copy of "Map 'n' Facts: Middle East" will be needed by you, the leader, and should be hung during the course in the room where the group meets. Order the videos "Celebration of Life" and "After the Storm" or reserve them from a resource center. (See the inside back cover for description of these resources and ordering information.)

3. Reserve other videos, films, filmstrips as soon as possible to be sure of their availability. A Filmography appears in the Resource Section on page 58.

4. Read through the entire course and get a feel for it as a whole. Mark ideas that particularly appeal to you and make notes of items for which advance planning is necessary. There are some items that must be duplicated and you will need to make arrangements for this. If your group did not engage in the previous study of Islam, also available from Friendship Press, you might want to substitute a session on this topic or simply to add a session at some point in the study (see page 60).

Write down your own goals for the course, using the objectives in this book as your guide.

5. Take time to read through the Resource Section beginning on page 29. Mark those ideas that interest you. Plan to include some cultural materials, such as a language lesson, some proverbs, or a sampling of Middle Eastern food as often as you can. Some suggestions are given in the session outlines but feel free to select other materials that fit your goals or your group better.

6. Read *Angle of Vision* by Charles Kimball yourself and plan how you will build its informa-tion and ideas into the goals of your course. The study sessions do not follow the sequence of the book exactly, but they offer opportunities to deal with most of its chapters. Each study session suggests an appropriate reading assignment from the book. The more people who have done this background reading, the livelier and more well informed the study sessions will be.

7. Start saving magazine and newspaper clippings about the Middle East, especially those about religious groups in the region. Look for variety in the countries represented. Plan a display board of clippings and pictures for the room where the group will meet. If you know any of the participants in advance, encourage them to start saving clippings also.

8. Write your denomination's office on Middle East affairs and obtain whatever resolutions, statements and other resources they have on the Middle East. Find out about cooperative efforts with churches and service projects in the Middle East as well. See the Resource Section for many of these addresses.

9. Check with your regional denominational office to see if they have speakers available on Middle East issues or if they know of Arab, Arab Canadian or American, or other Middle Eastern Christians in your area. Plan to include a speaker in one session or in an extra session, if you have time. Since Middle East issues are very volatile, it would better to invite speakers one at a time unless you have an experienced moderator who can manage a panel discussion.

10. Have such basics as newsprint, markers, masking tape, writing paper and pencils available for every session.

11. Remember! You can't use all of the materials suggested in this guide. Choose what you think will benefit your own group.

Note: Items that may be photocopied or otherwise duplicated for group use during the study are marked by a ☆. Other items are copyright, by Friendship Press or by other publishers as noted, and may not be reproduced without permission.

Session One
Facts and Feelings

Preparation

Before the Session

Bold letters in brackets designate activity in the Session Outline.

- Reread Chapter 1 in *Angle of Vision*.
- Choose some phrases in a Middle Eastern language to use in the session. (See Resource Section, page 52) **[A]**
- Duplicate a Facts and Feelings chart from page 6 for each member of the group. Duplicate the definitions from page 7 on separate sheets of paper. **[B]**
- Duplicate copies of "Hollywood's Arab," page 8, for your group. **[C]**
- Duplicate the blank map of the Middle East (see Resource Section, page 36). Have the Middle East "Map 'n' Facts" or another map available to post at the appropriate time during the session. **[E]**
- Collect newspaper editorials or magazine articles to use in the critical reading activity. It would be helpful to obtain several copies of those you wish to use. If you wish to duplicate an article you will need to obtain permission from the publisher first. **[F]**
- If you show the video "After the Storm" in this session as an introduction to the Middle East, see Activity D in Session Two.

Objectives

- To introduce the study.
- To explore the information and misinformation that participants already have.
- To talk about stereotypes and prejudices about the Middle East, and especially about Arabs, that are commonly held.

- To give participants tools for reading and listening more critically to news and information about the Middle East.

Session Outline

A. Introduction

Welcome the members of the group using words of greeting in Arabic or another Middle Eastern language. Ask people to introduce themselves by telling their name and giving a one-phrase descriptive image of the Middle East. Give an overview of the course and, in particular, of this session. Why are we studying the Middle East? Use the goals for the course that you developed (page 2, number 4). Also see the Introduction to this study guide and Chapter 1 of *Angle of Vision*.

B. Identifying stereotypes of the Middle East

Pass out the Facts and Feelings chart on page 6, which you have duplicated in advance, to members of the group.

Participants are to work alone and write in the "feelings" column how the word makes them feel when they first read it. When they finish the entire list, they should then begin again and write in the "facts" column a definition of the term. If they do not know the meaning, encourage them to note some elements they think might belong to its definition.

Gather in groups of three (triads) and talk about those words that brought out the strongest feelings in each participant. Discuss: What are those feelings? Why do you think you have them?

Call the group together and ask each triad to name the words that brought out the strongest feelings. Write them on newsprint and see if there are any commonalities. Is there any word or are there several words to which most of the group brings negative feelings? Positive feelings?

Pass out sheets with the definitions of the words (page 7). Ask the members of the group to spend a moment checking the definition of words about which they had strong feelings. Let several persons mention words that they had not defined correctly.

C. The Arab in the media

Pass out copies of the article titled "Hollywood's Arab: Still Stuck in the Desert" in the box on page 8. Let one person read it aloud.

Have members of the group recall movies, comic strips or television programs they have seen that portray Arabs. To what extent does the article truly describe what they saw? If someone is in doubt about whether a negative stereotype was portrayed, have the person imagine people from another ethnic or religious group, such as Irish Catholics, American Jews, or Black Protestants, in the scene instead of the Arab characters. Would the portrayal be acceptable then? Why or why not?

Many people believe that the United States has a long history of bigotry and prejudice against ethnic, religious or racial groups and that stereotyping is nothing new. There are about three million Arab-Americans in the U.S. and 250,000 to 300,000 Arab-Canadians. Many of them see the mass media as the major source of the problem of prejudice. What other sources do you see for this bias?

D. The baggage we each bring

In *Angle of Vision*, Charles Kimball says, "As Western Christians, we carry considerably more intellectual and emotional baggage than we realize. Our angle of vision has been shaped, and sometimes confused, by a variety of connections with this region of the world" (page 2). Be ready to take notes on newsprint as you ask the group to brainstorm a list of "baggage" that they bring to a study of the Middle East. What confuses them on the issues? How do they think

they developed their stereotypes? Be sure the group includes the areas that Kimball points out in Chapter 1; for example, the attachment to the Holy Land that is rooted in our religious history (page 6) and the tendency to know a host of details and remain ignorant of the broader context (page 10).

E. Mapping the Middle East

Pass out the blank map of the Middle East with the alphabetical list of countries (page 36). Ask participants to label the map with the names of the countries. When they have finished, hang up "Map 'n' Facts: Middle East" and review the placement of each country. Who got the most right? How many capitals and other major cities can the group locate?

F. Reading the news of the Middle East

This study guide and *Angle of Vision* by Charles Kimball were written during the immediate aftermath of the 1991 Gulf War. No book can keep up to date with the changes that might be taking place in this area of the world. It will be up to leaders and group members to read the news and current books to look for important developments.

Much that you will read, including newspaper articles and books are written from biased positions. The Middle East in particular has been reported from a Western and non-Muslim bias. For example, we have become accustomed to hearing the expressions "Muslim terrorist" or "Arab terrorism," even though terrorism is neither confined to those groups nor more prevalent in them. A recent Islamic summit has even condemned terrorism as contrary to the teachings of Islam. Other material that you read might be very anti-Jewish or anti-Israeli in its bias. Strong feelings have generated much writing and speaking that is clearly prejudicial against other ethnic or national groups. For example, you might find anti-Turkish materials written by Armenians conditioned by their history. It is important, then, to read with a critical eye.

Give your group practice in reading Middle Eastern news critically. Using newsprint or a blackboard, help your group understand the following elements they need to look for:*

1. Look for the self-interest of the author. From whatever information you have, see if you can make any guesses. What country is the writer from? What religious group? Does she or he represent a government or a political party? Does the basic approach of the publication itself serve some self-interest that has to be taken into account in reading?

2. Distinguish between fact and opinion. A factual statement can be proved, and opinion cannot. But not all factual statements are necessarily true, because they may be based on false or inaccurate information. Especially in the area of Jewish-Arab differences, selective historical memory has been the norm for much of the writing. In other words, true information is included or omitted according to whether it reinforces one's position or not.

3. Distinguish between opinions based on reason and opinions based on bias. Not all opinions are equal in value, and prejudice and emotion can be the motivating force in some opinions. In order to accept or reject those opinions, it helps to understand what point of view the author is trying to persuade readers to accept and what her or his motivation might be.

Give each person a copy of a newspaper editorial or a part of a magazine article. Several different pieces might be used but at least two people should have each piece. Have each person read the article and mark parts of it with an "F" for facts; "R" for an opinion based on reason; "B" for opinion based on bias, prejudice, or emotion; "I" for impossible to judge.

After a time of working alone, let each person find a partner with the same article and com-

---

* Activity based on "A 'Points of View' Approach," Arab World Notebook, edited by Shabbas, Audrey, and Al-Qazzaz, Ayad. (Berkeley, CA: Najda: Women Concerned About the Middle East, 1989), pages 67-69. Reprinted with permission.

pare what they have marked. Talk with each other about the possible self-interest of the author and how it affects the writing. If there is time, discuss the findings with the whole group. Be sure people can defend their reasons for marking articles as they did. Comment on how difficult a task it is to discover bias and on how this exercise can help group members deal with all kinds of material they read with a higher level of awareness of bias.

If your group is interested, ask people to take responsibility for reading articles about the Middle East in specific newspapers and magazines over the course of the study. Although a bit more difficult, this exercise can also be used with radio and TV programs. Using the criteria above, have members of the group report back in Sessions Four and Six about the kinds of bias they have found.

G. Conclusion

Ask people to write their names on their Facts and Feelings papers and collect them for use in Session Six. Let people keep the sheet of definitions. Give an overview of the remaining sessions and check the dates and times with the group. Ask people to bring articles to post on the bulletin board. Assign Chapter 1 in *Angle of Vision* to be read by the next session. Ask five persons each to prepare a two-minute report on one of the historical periods sketched out in the section "A Brief Historical Overview" in *Angle of Vision* (pages 15-23). The focus of the report is to be on what is important about that period for understanding events today. The areas to cover are: early Christianity, councils and divisions, Islam, the crusades, the Ottoman empire to the present.

Conclude with worship. Read 2 Corinthians 5:16-21 and ask people to tell some ways the study of the Middle East relates to the ministry of reconciliation Christ has called us to. End with the Litany for Peace and Justice on page 30 of the Worship Resources.

The Middle East: Facts and Feelings

Word	Feelings	Facts
Allah		
Arab		
bedouin		
belly dancing		
emir		
Islam		
jihad		
Middle East Christians		
Muslim		
PLO		
Qur'an		
Semitic		
sheikh		
Zionism		

Middle East Definitions

Allah The word for "God" in Arabic.

Arab A person whose native tongue is Arabic and who identifies with other Arabs as members of an ethnic group. This is not a religious group but a linguistic group.

bedouin A nomadic Arab desert dweller. Only a small percent of Arabs are bedouins.

belly-dancing A form of folk dancing engaged in by both men and women, it has been distorted into an entertainment form.

emir A paramount leader among several bedouin tribes.

Islam "Submission" to God or total commitment to the authority and power of God. The faith, submission and practice of the Muslim people.

jihad "Struggle" or "effort" in the path of God. It can be used to describe a personal internal struggle but it is sometimes used to describe a defensive "just war" to protect the interest of Islam. Mistakenly called a "holy war."

Middle East Christians The approximately twelve million Middle Easterners claiming allegiance to the Christian faith. Many are members of the oldest churches in Christianity and make up a 7 to 8 percent minority in the Middle East.

Muslim One who is submitted to God; one whose religion is Islam.

PLO Short for the Palestine Liberation Organization, a group formed in 1964 by Arab heads of state. Now the umbrella organization for most Palestinian political, economic, social and military organizations, the PLO is considered a government in exile by the Palestinian people.

Qur'an "Recitation" in Arabic; the book containing the messages from God recited by Muhammad and recorded by his followers. It is occasionally spelled "Koran."

Semitic Refers to a family of related Middle Eastern languages, including Hebrew, Arabic, Aramaic, and others.

sheikh Literally, "one who is old." A bedouin sheikh is the head of a tribe; a religious sheikh is a scholar learned in the Qur'an.

Zionism The movement to create or maintain a Jewish state through political means. It takes its name from Mount Zion, the hill in Jerusalem on which King David's palace is said to have stood.

★

Hollywood's Arab:
Still Stuck in the Desert

For years moviegoers have been offered stereotypical images of the Arab. The stereotype provides myths and misperceptions which tend to influence public opinion and limit the formulation of a successful policy in the Middle East.

The Arab male is portrayed as a contemptible character—cowardly, primitive, ignorant, cruel, vicious, lecherous and, often, fabulously wealthy. An Arab woman is either a sensuous belly dancer, whore, terrorist or a veiled, silent appendage to her husband.

Filmmakers too often dip into their script bags for the "Instant Arab Kit." For women, it contains belly dancers' outfits and veils; for men, it consists of *kuffiyahs*, flowing robes, sunglasses, scimitars, limousines and camels. Oil wells, sand dunes and *souks* set the scene.

In many films released in the mid-1980's, the Hollywood Arab prowls the screen amidst a mishmash of misinformation. Viewers see a disturbing recurrence of similarly negative characters, with inaccurate or stereotypical settings. The interchangeable sets of "Arabland" invariably show Israeli and American actors as veiled women in black, shabbily dressed men, ferocious terrorists, belly dancers, armed guards and evil dictators. The desert set offers a similar cast of characters, including sheep, horses and camels. Into the perennial desert the producers drop a military air base or a cheap mockup of an Arabian Nights' palace. Urban settings offer sheikhs in sunglasses doing dastardly deeds in black limousines or glittering Mercedes. Producers fail to show today's Arabian cities. Their message is: You can take the Hollywood Arab out of the desert, but you can't take the desert out of the Hollywood Arab.

Stereotypes form "pictures in our heads," and pictures relay powerful messages. Concerned moviemakers could channel such messages in a constructive or entertaining manner. But films cannot be entertaining or their messages constructive when a people is dehumanized.

(This article by Jack G. Shaheen is excerpted from *The Mideast Monitor* and appears in *Media & Values*, Spring, 1988, page 14). Used by permission of *The Mideast Monitor*.

Session Two
Long Religious Memories

Preparation

Before the session

Bold letters in brackets designate activity in the Session Outline.

- Reread Part I in *Angle of Vision,* especially "A Brief History of the Churches."
- Choose a technique and gather materials to make a time line. There are several ideas below in **[A]**.
- Plan to serve a Middle Eastern snack during the period spent working on the time line. *Lebneh* or *Hummus bi Tahini* with pita (pocket) bread would be easy to prepare and, if you provide plenty of napkins, shouldn't disturb the project.
- If you haven't learned at least one word in Arabic and one in Hebrew, plan to do so in this session **[B]**. See the Resource Section, page 52.
- Bring medium-size file cards for each member of the class. **[F]**
- If you will be using "After the Storm" in this session, preview the video and have equipment in place to show it **[D]**.
- Make two copies of the interview from Session Three (pages 14-15) to give those who volunteer to read it at the next meeting.

Objectives

- To relate historical events in the Middle East to those in the West and to review the relevant historical periods.
- To learn how history affected and still affects inter-religious relationships.

Session Outline

A. As people arrive: time line

Have the makings of a time line (see ideas below) and ask participants to place Middle East events in their proper place on the line. As a resource for this, use the time line in the "Map 'n' Facts," choosing only major events. Whatever technique you use for constructing the time line, your preparation should include a line with centuries and familiar events from European and North American history marked on it.

Some possible techniques for time lines:

1. Obtain a long piece of shelf paper and simply draw a line the length of the paper with a marker. Hang it vertically or horizontally according to your space. Measure off equal segments for centuries beginning with 2000 B.C.E. and mark them. You may want to use the more scholarly designations of B.C.E. (Before Common Era) and C.E. (Common Era) rather than B.C. and A.D., since both Muslims and Jews have their own dating systems beginning from important events in their own histories. Add the events in other parts of the world in a different color. Provide several markers of a third color for Middle Eastern events.

2. String a clothesline across the room or along a wall. Mark the centuries with colored tape, pieces of yarn or key tags. Provide pieces of paper and clip clothespins to add significant events in their proper places. Instead of clip clothespins you could use paper clips.

3. If you have a long bulletin board, put a piece of black tape across it and mark the centuries with vertical slips of paper. Furnish small file cards and tacks for the addition of Middle Eastern events.

B. Introduction

If you have been learning some words in other languages, be sure you have included both Arabic and Hebrew at this point. Review the time line the group has constructed, noting especially the relationship between Middle Eastern events and other more familiar events. Outline the plans for today's session.

C. Religious history in the Middle East

Remind your group that not all issues can be reduced to religious differences and that not all members of ethnic groups share the same religious affiliation. On the other hand, the Middle East cannot be comprehended without an understanding of religious history and feelings. Ask the individuals who have been assigned in advance to give two minute reports from *Angle of Vision* to sit together as a panel. As each of them reports, they should show on the time line when these events were happening. In addition, they should refer to the historical maps on "Map 'n' Facts."

D. View videocassette, "After the Storm."

"After the Storm: Power and Peace in the Middle East" is a 28-minute video that could be shown at any of several points during the course. You could also divide the video into two or three segments and show these in separate sessions.

The first two sections of the video fit the emphasis of Session Two especially well. Consider viewing the video as an activity in Session Two or in a separate session between Sessions Two and Three. (In such a "video viewing session," you could also show "Celebration of Life" in preparation for Session Three. See that session for a description.)

"After the Storm" provides a great deal of background information in a brief format. It will reinforce and supplement the information the group already has gained from the time line and the short reports. It is helpful in emphasizing a "long view" of religious and political histories—which often are inseparable in the Middle East. The video also highlights the difficulties and benefits of good relations between believers in three different monotheistic religions.

After the video, ask the group for brief responses: "What new item of information seemed most important to you? What region of the Middle East or period of its history would you like to learn more about?" If you are using the video in a session with more time for discussion, consult the guide that is packaged with the video for possible topics.

E. The past a part of today

At the end of the presentation or the video, divide the class into three sub-groups. Assign one sub-group each to represent Christians, Jews and Muslims. They are to think about the historical outline presented by the panel and ask themselves, "How would our constituency view the birth of Christianity, the spread of Islam, the crusades, the founding of the state of Israel, the Ottoman Empire, the Gulf War?" After a few minutes for discussion, let each sub-group report.

As a whole group discuss: In light of what you know about the religious history of the area, why might Muslims in the Middle East call the United States' intervention in the Persian Gulf War in 1991 "The New Crusade"?

F. Interfaith relationships

Have the sub-groups reconvene in their roles representing one of the religions and give each group two pieces of newsprint and markers. On one piece of newsprint they are to write the word "barriers" and list those things that get in the way of positive relationships with the other two religious faiths. On the second sheet of newsprint the sub-group is to write "encouragements" and list the things that support and promote positive relationships with the other two religious faiths.

Return to the total group and place all the "barrier" sheets together in one area and the "encouragements" in another area on the wall. Compare the viewpoints and identify which items are actually religious and which are political, cultural or economic.

Some of the **encouragements** your group might identify are:

- All three religions believe in one God and a life of prayer and worship.
- The religions all have scriptures and prophetic voices.
- They all trace themselves back to Abraham and revere many of the same ancestors in the faith. All are concerned with persons in the Hebrew Bible or Old Testament. Muslims also revere Jesus and Mary although they reject the divinity of Christ as well as the resurrection.
- The people all did live together as neighbors during some periods in the past.
- All three have some similar moral and ethical teachings

Some of the **barriers** might include:
- There is a history of military conquests and the wielding of political and economic power over one another.
- Each group has been isolated culturally from the others.
- Each group experiences minority status in one place or another.
- In Israel, Arabs have a second-class status and in the Occupied Territories both Christians and Muslims relate to Jews as occupiers.
- They have three different weekly Holy Days: Fridays for Muslims, Saturdays for Jews, Sundays for Christians.
- They see weakness and error in one another's theologies.
- Issues emerge around being a successor religion (Christianity to Judaism and Islam to Christianity).

- Each religion is experiencing a conservative resurgent or "back-to-basics" type of movement that tends to emphasize its own feelings of superiority and distance from others.

G. Jerusalem as holy for three faiths

Charles Kimball tells us that "Jerusalem, the 'city of peace,' stands at the symbolic center, the converging point for the three great monotheistic communities" (page 3). Give each participant a medium-size file card. Tell them to pretend it is a picture post card and that they are in Jerusalem. Have them write or draw what would be on the picture side and write a message home in the message space. Share the cards in any way you wish.

H. Conclusion

Assign the group to read Chapter 2 in *Angle of Vision*. Two people need to prepare to read the interview in Session Three and several others should work on reports on the families of churches. The reports will be a review of what others read and should simply help everyone to fill in the charts. (See Session Three outline.)

Worship today will focus around Jesus weeping over the city of Jerusalem. Begin with "A Prayer Before Reading the Scriptures" on page 34 of the Worship Resources. Read Luke 19:41-44. Ask the group to speak about what they think Jesus would be weeping for in our day. Pray for those things spoken about by the group.

Christians Who Call God "Allah"*

*"Allah" is "God" in Arabic. Middle Eastern Christians who speak other languages of course have other words for "God".

Preparation

Before the Session

Bold letters in brackets designate activity in the Session Outline.

- Reread Chapter 2 in *Angle of Vision*.
- Duplicate for each member of your group the church "families" chart on page 35. This is the same chart used in *Angle of Vision*. [B]
- Duplicate sufficient copies of the Church History Comparison Chart, page 16, for each participant. [B]
- In preparation for Activity D write one or two of the proverbs from the Resource Section (page 46) on each of several file cards. You will need at least as many cards as there will be people in your group. [D]
- If you will be using "Celebration of Life" in this session, preview the video and have equipment in place to show it. [G]
- At the end of this session, you will be halfway through. Refer to the section on Additional Learning Experiences and Settings (page 27) for ideas you might still include.

Objectives

- To learn about the various indigenous and implanted Christian communities in the Middle East.
- To explore ways that Christians work together in the Middle East.
- To understand the issues that are unique to Middle East Christians and to appreciate and empathize with the circumstances they find themselves in.

Session Outline

A. Introduction

Talk about the meaning of the word "Allah," which is an Arabic word meaning "God." It is used not only by Arab Muslims but by Arab Christians as well. Other language groups have other words that mean "God." Remind people that the Middle East is the birthplace of Christianity and share with your group the experience the author recounts in the Introduction of this guide. Ask the group: "What does it mean to be 'the continuous incarnation of Christ in the area'?"

Remind your group that at the end of this session, you will be at or near the middle point of the study. Further study and action concerning this region will depend on what members of this group plan. Begin a newsprint listing of ideas they might have for ways in which your group can follow through on what has been learned. Suggest that they look in Chapter 4 of *Angle of Vision* for some ideas. The list should be kept in the room where the group meets and worked on during each session.

Explain to the group what you will be doing in the remainder of the session.

B. The Middle Eastern families of churches

Hand out copies of the chart from page 35 (also shown in *Angle of Vision*, page 33) showing the history of Christian churches in the Middle East and a copy of the comparison chart on page 16. People who have been assigned to report on the various families of Christian churches should do so, pointing out the particular family of churches on the chart. Have group members fill in the Church History Comparison chart for themselves as reports are given.

Engage the group in a discussion what the word "missionary" means to each of the families of churches. Remind them of the fact that the relatively recent Protestant missionaries in the area came to convert the Muslims but instead often drew their membership from other, indigenous Christian groups.

C. Ecumenical relations in the Middle East

There is an excellent description in *Angle of Vision* (pages 40-55, especially pages 53-55) of the ways in which churches and para-church groups do and do not work together in the Middle East. Have your group discuss this with these questions:

What is your own experience with para-church organizations in North America?

Why do you think para-church groups are so active in the region? What do they contribute positively to the area?

What do you see as the greatest danger presented by para-church organizations?

Why is cooperative work so essential in the Middle East?

D. Sharing some proverbs

This session is heavy on factual learning, so a good break would be to spend time exploring some Middle Eastern proverbs. Introduce the activity by explaining that Middle Easterners make abundant use of proverbs; a person's wisdom and insight are demonstrated by his or her knowledge and use of proverbs. Give each person a file card with one or two proverbs written on it. Then have the members of the group walk around asking others if they can think of a common Western proverb that expresses the same idea. It is possible to come up with more than one idea. After a few minutes have people share their proverbs, both Middle Eastern and Western.

E. Living as a Christian in the Middle East

Have two members of your group read the interview on pages 14-15. It contains much information about living as a Christian minority in the Middle East.

After the interview is over, talk about the issues Laila points out. What are some difficulties of living as a member of a minority religion? Do you think Muslims in North America experience any of the same issues? Give examples.

F. Christianity: a future in the Middle East?

Pope Paul VI said, "Jerusalem without Christians would be merely a museum of Christianity." That is true of many areas of the Middle East that were important to early Christianity.

Have the class speculate about the choice they would make if they were Christians in the Middle East. Would they stay or emigrate and why? Put the words "stay" and "go" on newsprint and summarize the arguments for the group as they discuss the issue. What kind of a future does Christianity have in the Middle East?

G. View videotape, "Celebration of Life"

This 28-minute video is especially illustrative of some emphases in Session Three. It offers short glimpses of the worship life and the service ministries of Middle Eastern Christians in several countries. If the group will see this video in a special session or has 15 to 20 minutes for discussion afterwards, use the guide that is packaged with the video to plan the discussion.

If your schedule permits only brief responses, ask some questions like these:

- What interested you most about the worship services you saw? What seemed most different from worship in your church? What seemed most similar?
- What other image from the video most impressed you? Why?
- What word or phrase would you use to describe first the difficulties, then the opportunities, for members of the churches you saw in Syria? in Egypt?

H. Conclusion

Many church people who travel in the Middle East are asked a very important question by Christians they encounter. They are reminded that Jews around the world support the Jews who live in the State of Israel and that Muslims feel a sense of worldwide community. (It is known as the *umma*, the community of believers.) Then Christians are asked, "Why doesn't the worldwide Christian community support Christians in the Middle East?" How would your group members answer that question?

Ask members of the group to read Chapter 3 in *Angle of Vision* for the next session.

As you begin worship, remind the group that unity is often difficult to achieve. Speak together of the problems and joys of working on Christian unity in your own community. Join in the Litany of Confession on page 32 of the Worship Resources. End with the reading of Ephesians 4:1-6 (one Lord, one faith, one baptism).

Interview

BETTY: I want to thank you for this opportunity to talk with you, Laila. How long has your family been Christians?

LAILA: I am one of the Christians who can say that we trace ourselves back to the very beginning—the beginning of Christianity in the whole world. We can trace our own Church back to the apostles. We are ancient churches but we are not just dead stones in buildings and shrines; we are living stones, just as the Bible says. Have you visited many churches on your trip?

BETTY: Yes, I have been visiting churches, though I must admit that many of them are a bit strange looking to my eyes. They are so elaborate in comparison to my church at home.

LAILA: Worship in my church is very rich. Of course, many of our churches don't have the money to buy the finest of icons but those we have are beautiful to me. Through the eyes of the icon I can see the gaze of Christ. Isn't that beautiful in itself? Come to church and worship with me on Sunday. Experience our worship and see how we are happy to welcome you.

BETTY: Thank you, I will. We often hear of difficulties between religious groups in the Middle East. Is it difficult to live as a Christian in an area in which most people are Muslim?

LAILA: Christians, Muslims and Jews in the Middle East have lived together in a friendly fashion in the past although sometimes, in some periods of history, this broke down and we fought and killed each other. But mostly we Christians, and the Jews, too, have been tolerated by Muslims because we are "People of the Book." The Qur'an requires Muslims to accept "the religions of the Book"—in other words, Christians and Jews—and to provide protection for these religions.

Of course, there is a problem if the society is based on Islamic law (*shari'a*), because then non-Muslims are to be treated as *dhimmi* or protected citizens. That means we are free to practice Christianity and even to be governed by our own religious laws, but our rights and privileges are restricted. *Dhimmi* status comes at the price of payment of a special tax to the majority society and a prohibition against sharing our faith with non-Christians. In the past when this was true, it made us very isolated socially as well and limited our participation in the economic life.

BETTY: Well, how did you express your Christian life then?

LAILA: Worship, of course, was the center of our Christian lives and we engaged in serving others. Service can be a way of witnessing, too, especially when it means better schools or health care for people. Jesus called us to live out a ministry of reconciliation, just as you also talk about in the West.

BETTY: Do you ever feel close to Western Christians?

LAILA: Sometimes I really feel caught in the middle. I have to explain to you Western Christian about who I am and how my church differs from yours. We see

14

ourselves more as a community with an ethnic or cultural background than you do. We also are minorities and so continuity is of greater importance than change to us. And I also have to interpret myself to Muslims so that we can cooperate on building up our society. I don't want our society to be based on Qur'anic tolerance and protection, nor do I want religious conflict. I want our society to be based on mutual respect of religious and cultural identity.

BETTY: Has this caused you any difficulties lately?

LAILA: I have certainly had problems with being a Christian during the War in the Persian Gulf. Some of my Muslim acquaintances accused me of being an American. When your newspapers caricatured Muslims or made the war sound like a battle of the Christian West against the Muslim East, we Arab Christians had a hard time. People who weren't our friends even called us Christians "Crusaders."

BETTY: I hear Christians have been leaving the Middle East in large numbers. Do your difficulties ever make you feel like leaving the area?

LAILA: Well, I do have a good education and could find a place within your American society, I am sure. I even speak English quite well, don't you think? And I have considered emigration for I know my cousins in Detroit would help me. There is unrest here and the opportunities for me are more limited than they would be other places partly because I am a Christian. I probably won't ever have a job that uses my skills or what I have studied at university. It is very attractive to think about leaving.

BETTY: Do you suppose you will leave?

LAILA: No, I don't think so. We Arab Christians have survived in the past and will in the future. I am proud to be an Arab and to claim Arab culture as my own and I am proud to be a Christian and part of the Christian presence in the birthplace of Christianity. I want to preserve the traditions of my church and help people remember them.

BETTY: Thanks so much for this conversation. I will attend worship with you on Sunday. What time should we meet at the church?

☆

Church History Comparison Chart

Family Name	Churches	Countries	% of M.E. Christians	Origin in M.E.
Oriental Orthodox				
Eastern Orthodox				
Catholic				
Protestant and Anglican				
Assyrian Church of the East				

East Meets West Meets East

Preparation

Before the session

Bold letters in brackets designate activity in the Session Outline

- Reread Chapter 3 of *Angle of Vision*.
- Review the Resource Section and prepare to teach some more words in other languages to your group. Try words in some lesser known language this time. **[A]**
- For Activity B, plan for readers for the folk tales (see Resource Section, pages 42-45). If you will use a storyteller, help that person prepare. **[B]**
- For Activity D1, write large on newsprint the causes of unrest and instability discussed in *Angle of Vision* on pages 56-75 and identified below in Activity **D1**.
- For Activity D3, if you will be passing out copies of the profiles of "peace people," (pages 37-38), duplicate them for your class. **[D3]**
- Copy profiles of women from the Resource Section, pages 39-41, to give volunteers to prepare for Session Five.
- Copy recipes to give to volunteers to prepare for Session Five.

Objectives

- To expand awareness and appreciation of Middle Eastern perspectives and cultures through folk tales.
- To explore some of the political issues in the Middle East.
- To identify areas calling for the church to engage in peacemaking.

Session Outline

A. Introduction

Greet your group with some Arabic or Hebrew words that they have learned in previous sessions. Add some new vocabulary for them to learn.

Read (or paraphrase) the following to the group:

In his book *The Forest People*, Colin M. Turnbull describes his stay with the Pygmy people of the Belgian Congo (now called Zaire). Near the end of the visit, he took a young man, Kenge, out of the forest for the first time. Kenge had never seen a hill or open ground. When what he saw did not conform to his cultural mind set or could not be described within his language system, he believed it to be an untruth. "You liar!" he said, when he was told that the snow on the mountains was solid water. When he saw buffalo at a distance, he thought they were insects; on approach, as they seemed to get bigger and bigger, he held himself behind the closed windows of the car, and his comment was that they were not *real* buffalo.

We each grow in our own rain forest—with our own world view—and we hold on to the belief that the world is as we see it. If we are to become globally aware Christians, we must leave those rain forests and enter into other people's forests.

(From, "Discipleship Alive! Teacher Training and Pastor's Quarterly," Fall Year 3. Copyright 1990, Brethren Press. Used by permission.)

Ask people to briefly cite times when they had insight into another culture's perspective.

Introduce the outline of this session, stating that you will be both looking at the Middle East from some new perspectives and looking at some of the ties that bind us to that region.

B. Developing some new perspectives

Present one or more of the folk tales from the Resource Section (pages 42-45), to the group as whole, or, if you have obtained publishers' permission to reproduce them, in small groups. Since folk tales are meant to be heard rather than read, make as much use of oral presentations as possible. If you divide into small groups, let someone in each small group read one of the folk tales to their group. If someone is willing to work with the material in advance, that person could tell a story to the whole group.

After each story, list those insights the story gives about Middle Eastern culture. Which of these might be particularly valuable ideas for Western culture to incorporate?

C. Perspectives on the news

If you have members of the group reading articles with a critical eye for bias as suggested in Session One, have them give an interim report at this time. The focus could be the new perspectives on Middle East news reporting they have gained during this study.

D. Peacemaking through understanding

The material in Chapter 3 of *Angle of Vision* is wide ranging and detailed. There are several suggestions below for dealing with it. You should definitely do Activity 1, but you will probably have to choose between 2 and 3. If your group is very large, you might simply divide it up according to people's interests and pursue both subjects. All three activities could be used in an extended session.

1. Instability and Unrest

Place before your group the newsprint chart listing the sources of instability and unrest identified by Charles Kimball in *Angle of Vision*: A long history of foreign domination (pages 58-61); policies of unrepresentative governments (pages 61-64); differing visions for new societies (pages 64-65); great inequities in wealth and re-

sources (pages 65-66) and unresolved regional conflicts (especially pages 67-77). Ask the group to recall an example from each of the sources and then to add other illustrations from recent newspaper, radio and television news.

2. Lessons from the Gulf war

Have the group divide into dyads (groups of two) and share with each other the new insights about the Gulf War that they gained by reading the material in *Angle of Vision*. Which of the sources of instability and unrest identified in the Kimball book do they see as important to this particular insight? Have each dyad report on one insight and what they have identified as related sources of instability and unrest.

Events move on even after writers turn in their manuscripts, especially in a volatile area such as the Middle East. Are there new examples from the Gulf area illustrating the instability and unrest since these books have been written? Conclude this section by asking the question: "What does it mean to live as a Christian in an interdependent world?"

3. The Israeli/Palestinian Conflict

Have various participants read aloud the profiles of people who are working toward peace in the Israeli-Palestinian conflict (pages 37-38). What common threads do you see running through these stories?

Provide paper and pencils and have people meet in dyads. Have each dyad compose a telegram to one of the profiled people. Share these "telegrams" with the whole group.

E. Conclusion

Have the group summarize the session by finishing this sentence, "I stepped outside my own rain forest today when. . . ." Have people jot down their own words and then share them with the total group.

Add to your newsprint listing of ways to share the group's learning after the course is over (begun last session). There are some additional suggestions in Session Six (pages 25-26) which you might put on the list yourself at this time. Are there any ideas that individuals seem ready to commit themselves to? If so, let them make some plans and bring them to the group in Session Five or Six.

Suggest to your group that they watch for news items and other stories that reflect the sources of unrest and bring them to the next session.

If you are including Session Five on Women and the Family next, choose several people to prepare to share the biographical sketches. If they can "role play" to introduce themselves as those women, that would be particularly helpful. Ask for volunteers to prepare food from the Middle East to use in the coming session and give them copies of the recipes. If you choose to substitute another session from the Additional Learning Experiences (beginning on page 27), be sure to make the appropriate assignments.

For today's worship read Ephesians 2:13-22. Remind people of the issues the group has talked about today. Ask them to consider their relationship to the Middle East as you slowly reread the passage. Conclude with a prayer from the Worship Resources.

Session Five
Women and the Family

Preparation

Before the session

Bold letters in brackets designate activity in the Session Outline

- For Activity C, duplicate the paragraph on the family (page 22) for everyone. **[C]**
- Write the questions for Activity C on small file cards (3"x 5"). **[C]**
- Review the information on Arab names from the Resource Section, pages 50-51, and decide how to share it. **[D]**
- Reread the profiles of women that others will use and review the introductory pieces on those particular women, page 23, for your presentation. **[F]**
- Gather any serving or eating utensils needed if food is to be served.
- Remind yourself again that we are trying to appreciate and not make detrimental comparisons either in terms of Christians and Muslims or in terms of the West and Middle East. Enter this session with that goal clearly in mind.

Objectives

- To appreciate the high value placed on family in the Middle East.
- To understand the fears of many Middle Eastern people about the effects of Westernization and modernity on the family.
- To appreciate the various situations Middle Eastern women find themselves in and the strengths they bring to those situations.

Session Outline

A. As people arrive

Food and hospitality is important to Middle Eastern families, so it is appropriate to serve some food at the beginning of this session. See the Resource Section for recipes and information about food that you might share.

B. Introduction

If anyone has brought news items to illustrate the sources of unrest, let them share them at this time.

Remind participants of the cultural "rain- forests" talked about in Session Four. Ask them to recall any instances since the last session when they have experienced coming out of their own "rainforest." Tell them that today they will need to look beyond many of their Western ideas and explore some other "rainforests." Remind them that all religions and cultures have values and strengths. It is easy to criticize from the outside, but what we are looking for today are the unique strengths brought by families and women in the Middle East. Outline the session.

C. Inside the family

Introduce the subject by asking what "family" usually means in our North American context. Explain that the Arabic word for family, *ahl*, is a term that includes the extended family and distant relatives. In the Middle East the traditional family unit remains the basic unit of social organization, and it performs many of the functions that we expect of the nation-state.

Hand out copies of the paragraph in the box on page 22 describing the ideal of the Middle Eastern family and give people time to read it.

Ask people to find one other person to talk with (form dyads). They are to look at one current issue affecting Middle Eastern families and talk about how Western and Middle Eastern families might differ in their approach to it. Remind them that an important issue for the modern Middle Eastern family is to uphold both the development of the individual and the traditions of the family. Have the pairs pick their subject by random from cards on which you previously have written these questions:

1. How would care for the elderly be worked out?
2. What do you perceive the role of family planning might be? How would such decisions be made?
3. How does the education of women strengthen or weaken the family?
4. How does increased urbanization affect the family?
5. Women have always worked within or near the home, but now increasing number of women must go away from the home to work as well. What effects do you think this will have? How will the family maintain its sense of self?

Draw a line down the center of newsprint or a chalkboard. Mark one side "alike" and the other "not alike." Bring the group together and ask the dyads to report back to the whole group by describing which parts of family life in the two regions show similarities and which parts show differences.

D. Family names

Tell the group about the way names are often constructed in Arab countries. (See Resource Section, pages 50-51, for information.) Let each person work out what various names she or he could be called using this system. Go around the group and ask people to tell who they are by using these new names.

E. Ideas about women

As you take notes on a piece of newsprint, ask the group to brainstorm what images come to mind when people think of Middle Eastern women, Arab women, Turkish women, etc. Be sure people include such images as docile vic-

tim, shrouded non-entity, exotic sex symbol under a veil, one of many wives, part of a harem.

Then have the group talk about how North Americans have developed those images and where they have come from. Help the group to include:

- Folktales such as the *Arabian Nights*, which emphasize the exotic.
- Adventure stories written mostly from a male point of view. In these, women are almost never encountered as significant human individuals.
- Media that capitalize on the sensational and unusual. For example, much space was given in newspapers and magazines in 1990 to the Saudi Arabian women who were denied driver's licenses, but in most countries of the region, women can and do drive.

F. Getting to know some women

Remind your group of the family issues discussed earlier in the session. Remind them also that women in the Middle East are both rich and poor, from cities and villages, and a few are bedouins still. Some are well educated and other illiterate, and some women are traditional while others are quite Westernized. The Middle East is a male-dominated culture, but women of all religious groups play a variety of roles and work toward an increasingly important place within their culture. Quote Elizabeth Warnock Fernea's statement that the example of the West is no longer seen as the answer to problems.

People are attempting to improve their lives through indigenous traditions and customs; through the dominant religion of the area, Islam; and through their own kinship and family patterns. They are improving and combining the new and the old, adapting, changing and building, trying to create their own form of independence.*

Use the paragraphs on page 23, which give some basic information about women's lives, to

---

*Fernea, Elizabeth Warnock, *Women and the Family in the Middle East; New Voices of Change* (Austin, Texas: University of Texas Press, 1985), page 2.

make your own introduction to several Middle Eastern women. Have the people who have prepared in advance introduce themselves as these women or tell their stories. (The profiles themselves are found in the Resource Section, pages 39-41.) The group should look for the strengths these particular women bring to their lives and not make comparisons. Name some of these strengths after each profile. At the end the this activity, ask your group, "What can we learn from these women?"

G. Conclusion

Ask your group to read Chapter 4 of *Angle of Vision* and to think about ways to follow up on the course after it is completed, if they have not already done so. Review the ideas on the group's list and remind the group that Session Six will be the last chance to deal with these ideas.

For worship ask the members of the group to consider the gifts that women in the Middle East bring to their families, communities and the world. Tell them that they will be making up the prayer by praying about these gifts. When the group has had time to reflect, read 1 Corinthians 12:4-11, about varieties of gifts. Ask members of the group to end each petition with the words, "we pray," and respond as a group to each petition with the phrase, "Thank you, God" Begin the prayer with words such as:

Gracious God, we hold before you today the women of the Middle East of all religions and ages. For their gift of hospitality, we pray . . .
"Thank you, God."

Let other group members continue the prayer. End the prayer time with the Lord's Prayer.

Family in the Middle East

The family in the past (and, to a great extent, today) provided economic and emotional support to its members, which might consist of groups as small as 20 or as large as 200, for not only were mother, father and children included in the definition of the group, but also grandparents, uncles, aunts and cousins to several degrees on both sides of the marital connection. An individual . . ."inherited" his or her religious, class and cultural identity, which was reinforced by the customs and mores of the group. In exchange for the allegiance of its members, the group served as an employment bureau, insurance agency, child and family counseling service, old people's home, bank, teacher, home for the handicapped (including the insane), and hostel in time of economic need. Men and women both remained members of their natal families for all of their lives, even after marriage. A divorced woman returned to her natal family, which was responsible for her support until remarriage. A divorced man returned to his natal family, and his parents cared for his children. In exchange for these services, the individual members were expected to place the group's survival above their personal desires, especially at the time of marriage, and to uphold the reputation of the family by behaving properly and "maintaining the family honor."

From an article in the April, 1983, issue of *Discovery*, the research magazine of The University of Texas at Austin. Used by permission.   ☆

Introductions to Profiles

Introduction to Nawal el Saadawi. The status of women in the Middle East varies widely and it is a mistake to infer the status of all women from one country or one incident. In the past, kinship and family groups along with religious judges almost completely determined the rules that bound and controlled women. National law, though, has taken over to some extent, differing in policy from countries in which polygamy is legal and brides need not attend their own weddings to those where women have considerable marriage and divorce rights. Still, cultural constraints rather than religious beliefs or national laws define the limits on women. Nawal el Saadawi is a part of the small but growing feminist movement active in women's rights issues as well as working for improved public health and working conditions. Other women from more religiously oriented feminist movements among Christians, Muslims, and Jews are studying their own religious writings and calling attention to the cultural contexts in which these writings originated. They are also working to separate the influences that come from religion from those that come from culture.

Introduction to Umm Samir and Jamileh. Women have been moving out from the home in several ways in recent years. They are becoming more politically active and even in relatively conservative societies they may pass political information, preserve social interaction, hide weapons, and persuade their men to participate publicly. In some societies, as Jamileh's experience shows, women have participated in street politics by demonstrating and even taking up arms. In most cases, though, they still remain in secondary positions.

Women have always worked within the home and often have added agriculture and market sales to their private domain out of economic necessity. In recent years factory wage labor and, for educated women, medicine, teaching and other professional roles have taken more women into the public arena and given them a greater sense of self-worth. Laws and custom often still give the husband the right to grant or withhold permission for his wife to work. The manliness of a husband is thought to be reflected both in his capacity to provide for his wife and in his ability to claim authority over her. Tension is created in the family when male authority is thought to be challenged by women who work outside the home. Yet, as we see in Umm Samir, a woman of the West Bank, necessity often overrides preference.

Introduction to Farida. Just as some feminists have been challenging the continuing imposition of the veil, other women have been finding a new type of veiling through "Islamic" dress and head scarves. Although the Qur'an itself says nothing about veiling, it does urge women to dress modestly. Veiling has been more a matter of local custom, especially for upper and middle class women. In throwing off former colonial and Western ideas and ideals, men and women have looked for ways of expressing their new-found identities. In the Maghreb, the former French colonies in North Africa, wearing a scarf that covers the hair and neck and long sleeves to cover the arms are signs of pride for many women. On the other hand, when dress is imposed by conservative men as a political statement, as it is in the Gaza area, it becomes oppressive to many women. Farida sees her mode of dress as a sign of her religious beliefs and a part of the Islamic reform movement (see pages 64-65 in *Angle of Vision*).

Introduction to Maud. In each of the major religious groups—Muslims, Christians and Jews—there are women who give themselves wholeheartedly to their religious traditions. Some devote their lives to prayer and study; others serve as teachers, social workers, and leaders of organizations. All of them put service to their religion and their God above their own personal lives. Maud is one of a group of women in Lebanon who might be called Confessors of the Faith. This term is used for someone who suffers and witnesses to the faith under extreme conditions of hardship. ☆

Session Six
Hope for the Future

Preparation

Before the session

Bold letters in brackets designate activity in the Session Outline

- Reread Chapter 4 in *Angle of Vision*
- Review for yourself the Resource Section on language and prepare to teach at least one version of "good-bye" or "peace be with you." [B]
- Add other statements to the list in Activity C, "Christian stances," drawing from discussion during the previous sessions. [C]
- Duplicate materials you wish to share from your denominational offices. If there are pictures or articles that would make a good display, have materials on hand to encourage your group members to create the display as they arrive. [A, D]
- Find the Facts and Feelings Charts you saved from Session One. [G]
- Gather any materials you will need for the concluding sharing, such as construction paper and markers. [G]

Objectives

- To explore the various positions Christians are taking on the Middle East and see where your own position fits in.
- To learn about your denomination's stances and relationships with the Middle East.
- To look for signs of hope in people who are working toward peace in the Middle East.
- To plan for follow-up activities that will allow the group to share what they have learned.
- To conclude the course through a review of the feelings and learnings of the participants.

Session Outline

A. As people arrive

If the material you have from your denomination lends itself, have people make a display of the pictures and articles. Consider sharing it with your congregation.

B. Introduction

This is a good time to review all of the phrases in various languages you have been learning during this course. Be sure you have taught your group a parting greeting.

Outline the session and remind the group that this is the last official meeting.

C. Christian stances on Middle East issues

Christians have taken a variety of stances on issues concerning the Middle East. The purpose of this activity is to allow individual members of your group to express whether they agree or disagree with these stances. The best way is to clear a path in the classroom, designating one end as *agree* and the other as *disagree*. As you pose each statement, let people place themselves along the line from agree to disagree. Have them speak up about why they have placed themselves where they have before going on to the next statement.

Another technique is to read each statement and then allow people to raise their hands if they agree, then if they disagree, then if they are not sure. Record all the votes on newsprint and then ask people to tell why they chose their position. The drawback to this technique is that it is difficult to express degrees of agreement or disagreement.

Use the following statements and add others that you think of and that have come out of group discussion and your reading.

1. The issues in the Middle East are fairly simple and easy to sort out.

2. Western churches need to send missionaries to help the Middle Eastern churches convert more people to Christianity.

3. Ecumenism in the Middle East will help the churches preserve their individual identities.

4. The Holy Spirit is active in Islam as well as in Christianity.

5. The primary goal for Christians as minorities in a Muslim society is to witness to Christ.

6. Churches of the Middle East should withdraw from political and social involvement in order to preserve themselves as separate communities.

7. The presence of Arab-Christians in the United States and Canada makes Christian/Muslim dialogue more difficult.

8. God is more interested in Israel than in other countries.

D. Denominational positions on Middle East issues

Pass out copies of your own denomination's resolutions and position papers on the Middle East or summarize them for your group. Also tell them about people from your particular denomination who serve in the region and about ties to specific churches and denominations in the Middle East. In *Angle of Vision*, Charles Kimball talks about three areas of responsibility toward the Middle East as partnership in **ministry, education,** and **advocacy**. Divide into three groups, each taking one of these areas to look for in your denominational information. Have the sub-groups report back on how your denomination sees its mutual responsibility with Middle Eastern Christians.

E. Hope in the Hearts of People

During this study your group has encountered many people from the Middle East. In Session Four, they met several people concerned with peace in the Israeli/Palestinian conflict. In Session Three, Laila, a Christian, talked about her concerns, and in Session Five, various women were introduced.

Even though groups of people can be hopeful, it is also important for hope to be experienced by individual persons as a part of their own lives. Review and recall the Middle Eastern people you have encountered with the group and ask the questions: "Where do each of these people see hope and how do they experience it? What is it they hope for?"

F. What happens after the study is over?

It is hoped that your group, or some members of the group, will commit themselves to further study or action on the Middle East and the issues that have surfaced. Review the newsprint on which the group has been listing ideas that they think might be feasible. Be sure that the ideas in Chapter 4 of *Angle of Vision* and in this study guide have been included. After completing the list, encourage the group members to state their particular interest in specific ideas. If some people have already begun working, let them report at this time and engage others in their plans. Ask for volunteers to work on other ideas where people have shown interest or energy and get specific names and commitments. If there is time in the session, begin your planning. If not, be specific about when any committees or task groups will meet to plan. In addition to approaches in Chapter 4, some possibilities are:

1. Contact your local public schools and see what they teach about the Middle East and at what grade levels. Is the curriculum biased or fair toward all ethnic groups? If materials are not available for teachers on Arab culture, you might wish to recommend or provide such resources as:

Arab World Notebook (secondary school)
Edited by Audrey Shabbas and Ayad Al-Qazzaz.
Available for $39.95 from
NAJDA: Women Concerned About the Middle East
P.O. Box 7152
Berkeley, CA 94707

Arab World Almanac (available to secondary teachers)
3 issues per year, from
AMIDEAST
1100 17th St. NW
Washington, DC 20036

Middle East Gateway Series (intermediate grades)
Juanita W. Swedenburg, publisher
16195 East Carmel Drive
Fountain Hills, AZ 85268

2. Plan a sharing time with your own congregation. This could include worship that makes use of the worship resource section on pages 29-34. It could also include a supper with Middle Eastern food and a speaker. If you have a speaker, be sure to interview the person in advance to determine her or his biases and positions on issues of concern to your group. As mentioned in the Introduction, you might wish to have more than one speaker representing different perspectives. These guests should be invited for different occasions unless you have someone very experienced in arranging and moderating a panel. Your regional denominational office might have a list of speakers to help you.

3. Engage your local congregation in continually learning about your own denomination's involvement in the Middle East. The materials you have received could be made into a wall display or bulletin board exhibit if the group has not done this as people arrived today. Information could be placed in your newsletter or Sunday bulletins about advocacy networks and issues to write about in letters to members of Congress. Prayers for specific denominational representatives working in the Middle East could be included in worship services.

4. If people in the group were collecting news articles over the weeks, take time now to summarize the kinds of bias they have found in them. If appropriate, people can plan to write letters to the publishers expressing their concern about the biases they have found.

G. How have I changed?

Hand out the Facts and Feelings papers you saved from the Session One. Each person should look over the lists of words and the feelings they generated. Mark any words that seem different now and in the original triads share those changes.

H. Conclusion

Give each person a piece of construction paper or typing paper. Suggest that they write on their paper a few phrases about the most important things they have learned during this study of the Middle East. Provide markers in greens, yellows, blues and reds—the colors often used in Muslim prayer rugs. Have each person create a simple, colorful geometric border for her or his paper. Clear an open space on the floor and stand in a circle around it. Each participant then places his or her paper on the floor, naming the important things learned. Each paper should touch the others, forming a mosaic. (If the group is very small, provide several small pieces of paper to each person.)

Worship as the group gathers around the mosaic. Read 1 Peter 3:8-12 and ask people to state how they will "seek peace and pursue it" in days ahead. End with the Litany for Peace and Justice (Page 30 of the Worship Resources), the same litany used in Session One. Just before leaving, have everyone join together in speaking a word for "good-bye" or "peace be with you" in a Middle Eastern language.

Additional Learning Experiences and Settings

1. Beyond the TV map: countries we don't hear about on TV. Instead of studying Women and the Family for Session Five or for an additional session, a study of some lesser known countries of the Middle East would be interesting. Some basic information about the little-known country of Cyprus can be found in *Angle of Vision*, pages 31-32. At the previous session, assign each person one of the countries for research and reporting. Suggest that they use such resources as the "Map 'n' Facts," encyclopedias, the public library, etc. List the kinds of information that people should look for and report on. Areas could include: climate and terrain, natural resources, industries, exports and imports, average income, when formed as a nation-state and kind of government, original inhabitants and migration patterns, religious history, medical issues, educational issues, marriage and childraising customs, crafts.

At the session where people report, be sure to have a large map on the wall so speakers can identify the locations of their countries. It would be good to break up the session with some food, a folk tale or other cultural experience.

2. Many Christians in the Middle East are members of Orthodox Churches. If you are a Protestant or Roman Catholic group, take a field trip to an Orthodox Church. Sessions Two and Three of *Eyes To See, Ears To Hear: Study Guide to the Peoples and Churches of the USSR* (Friendship Press, see page 60)) contain information on Orthodox worship and spirituality and a guide to visiting Orthodox churches.

3. A session on Islam for those groups who have not studied this religion recently can be used as a substitute for Session Five on Women and the Family or in addition to the other six sessions. The 23-minute filmstrip, *Islam: An In-troduction*, plus discussion would be the easiest way to cover the material in one session. The filmstrip is available from: The Middle East Institute, 1761 N Street, N.W., Washington, DC 20036 (telephone: 202-785-2710).

Another way of exploring Islam briefly would be to select several activities from *One God, Two Faiths: Study Guide to the World of Islam* (Friendship Press; see page 60). You might also take a field trip to a mosque. Session Three in *One God, Two Faiths* contains suggestions for such a visit.

4. Explore ethnic pluralism. Groups such as the Armenians and Kurds form ethnic minorities that exist across national boundaries in the Middle East. Some information about the role of the Armenians appears in *Angle of Vision* on pages 28-29 and 60-61, and background on the Kurds on pages 60 and 68-69. Find more background information in encyclopedias, books and other materials on the Middle East from your local library. Be sure to explore enough history to discuss why these groups of ethnic minorities find themselves in several nations. You might like to debate the issue of whether such peoples should live in separate small countries of common ethnic cultures or not.

Adapting this Course for Other Times and Settings

The materials and sessions for this study can be adapted for formats other than a six-session course.

1. If you have fewer than six sessions, you will still want to include some of the Session One materials on "Facts and Feelings" and most of Session Three. From Session Four use only parts of Activity D, and skip Session Five. Conclude with Session Six.

2. If you have more than six sessions, you can incorporate some of the ideas listed above as well as use more time in planning and carrying out activities to share your learnings. A worship service or church-wide event ought to be included if possible.

3. A retreat can be planned using the study sessions. It is suggested that in addition to meals, recreation and free time, blocks of one to two hours be scheduled for study. You can use Session One on Friday evening and parts of Sessions Two and Three on Saturday morning. Session Four, along with recreational opportunities, including cooking Middle Eastern food, would be used on Saturday afternoon and Session Five on Saturday evening. Sunday morning should be devoted to worship and Session Six. If you cannot include cooking, plans could be made in advance for people to bring Middle Eastern desserts and snacks.

4. An intergenerational event or mission fair can be designed using the cultural materials and such activities from the session plans as: filling in the map; watching the videos; listening to folk tales; making a time line; presenting and discussing the interview; hearing about your denomination's involvements in the Middle East; and worshiping.

5. Youth classes or groups can use many of these study materials. It might be particularly interesting for them to explore their own school curriculum in terms of what ethnic materials are taught and how biased the curriculum materials are. Such things as the commemoration of different ethnic and religious holidays, the resources in the library, and the assembly programs are as important to look at as the classroom curriculum. See Session Six for suggested materials for schools.

Resource Section

Items in this section can be photocopied or otherwise duplicated for study group use, **except the five folktales on pages 42 and 44-45**. To reproduce any of those tales requires obtaining permission from the individual publisher. Please use items only for activities related to the Middle East study.

Worship Resources

Note: The issue of inclusive language has not been dealt with in the churches of the Middle East and, therefore, worship materials from that area will be problematic for many people and groups in the United States and Canada. As I compiled these worship resources I had to choose between using authentic materials written or actually used by Middle Eastern Christians or worship materials written by Westerners. I have chosen the former and recommend that those who use these materials make the changes necessary. When He, His or Him refers to the deity, the word "God" can be used instead. The words "Father" and "Lord" have been left without change although some readers might wish to add "and Mother" or other names for God. Some suggested changes appear in brackets.

BJB

The use of these worship resources

Worship is planned for the end of each session, and ideas for using some of the following materials are given at that point in the session activities. If your group chooses to share your study with the congregation during regular Sunday morning worship, it would be best to follow your church's usual order of service and incorporate the prayers, a litany, Scriptures, etc., in their common places.

If you are planning a worship service with a retreat or a special program, one possible order of service is:

Call to worship
Coptic Orthodox prayer that precedes worship (below)
Hymn such as "In Christ There is No East or West"
Scripture passage about peace
Sharing by members of group concerning our ties to the Middle East and Christian peacemaking
Scripture passage about church unity
Sharing by members of group on issues facing Christians
Prayer from the Old Syriac (page 32)
Hymn such as "Christ Has Called Us to New Visions" (page 33)
Litany for Peace and Justice (page 30)
Benediction

Prayers

Coptic Orthodox Prayer of Thanksgiving

This passage precedes all acts of worship.

O Master, Lord God, Almighty Father of our Lord, our God and our Savior Jesus Christ, we thank you in every condition, for any condition and in whatever condition. For that you have covered us, preserved us, accepted us, had compassion on us, sustained us, and brought us to this hour.

(Included in Carden, John, compiler. *With All God's People: The New Ecumenical Prayer Cycle*, 1989. Geneva: World Council of Churches, WCC Publications, page 4-5.)

Litany for Peace and Justice

(This litany was used for the opening service of the Week of Prayer for Christian Unity in St. George's Cathedral, Jerusalem, in 1988.)

The response to each petition, following the phrase "Let us pray to the Lord," is "Lord, have mercy."

In peace let us pray to the Lord,

That violence, oppression and injustice may cease from our land, while justice and peace flourish, let us pray to the Lord;

[Lord, have mercy]

That the pain of all who suffer in our land, Muslim, Jew and Christian, the grief of those who mourn, and the memories of those who cannot forget past hurt, may know his [God's] healing touch, let us pray to the Lord;

That across all barriers of race and creed we and all who dwell in our land may respect each other's dignity and seek to serve each other in love, let us pray to the Lord;

That our self-interest and self-concern which have increased our neighbors' bitterness against us may be forgiven, let us pray to the Lord;

That the barriers of hatred, suspicion, anger, greed and fear which divide the peoples of this land may be removed from our hearts and minds, let us pray to the Lord;

That all who are now in conflict in our land may renounce violence and seek peace by the way of love, let us pray to the Lord;

That we may put our trust in God and experience his [God's] deliverance, let us pray to the Lord;

That God's promise of justice and righteousness may become real for the peoples of this land, that they may live in freedom and peace, let us pray to the Lord;

That the Holy Spirit may work through our struggle and confusion to accomplish the Father's [Creator's] good purposes among us, let us pray to the Lord;

That the Holy Spirit may lead us from prejudice to truth and mercy, teach us truly to love our enemies, and deliver us from hatred and vengefulness, let us pray to the Lord;

That we may commit ourselves to establishing true peace and reconciliation in the unrelenting search for justice and a world order that is fair to the generations yet to be, let us pray to the Lord;

That there may be such unity in your Church that everyone may know that the Father has sent his [the] Son who truly dwells among us, let us pray to the Lord;

Lord, have mercy. Amen.

Used by permission of the Rt. Rev. Samir Kafity, President-Bishop, The Episcopal Church in Jerusalem and the Middle East.

An Introduction to the Lord's Prayer

From the Holy Mass according to the Armenian rite.

O God of Truth and Father of mercy. We thank you for the honor you bestowed on our sinful nature. Our forefathers [ancestors] call you their God but in your kindness you chose to be our Father. We beseech you Lord, make the Grace of Sonship [Grace], you bestowed on us [as sons and daughters], grow and flourish in your church every day, and grant that we may call upon you, with confidence, O heavenly Father, and pray as we sing: "Our Father who art in heaven. . . ."

(from the Worshipbook, Middle East Council of Churches Assembly, Cyprus, 1990, page 9, used by permission of the M.E.C.C.)

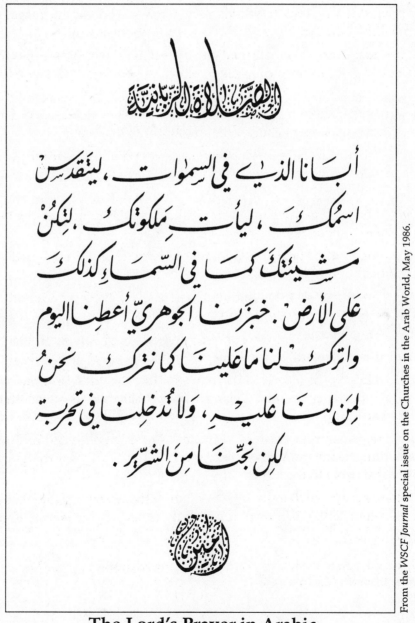

From the WSCF Journal special issue on the Churches in the Arab World, May 1986.

The Lord's Prayer in Arabic

Written in Farsi and Diwani calligraphy. (Arabic is read from right to left.)

A Litany of Confession

(The response to each petition is *"Kyrie Eleison,"* spoken three times. *Kyrie Eleison* is Greek and translates "Lord, have mercy.")

Brothers and sisters, we place ourselves before the word of the Apostle Paul addressed to the community at Ephesus, "to maintain the unity of the Spirit in the bond of peace." This word reveals to us that we have sinned against unity; that is why it leads us to ask for the Lord's forgiveness.

For our complacency with what we are and what we have, and our failure to open our eyes to recognize the values of others, Lord, have mercy on us.

For yielding to our impatience in dialogues with our brothers and sisters and for not having been willing to welcome them and listen to them and receive them, Lord, have mercy on us.

For having made no effort to understand the forms of thought, of witness to the Gospel and of spirituality which differ from ours; for not having had the courage to blend fraternal [sisterly and brotherly] love with the search for truth, Lord, have mercy on us.

For not having entered into a humble, confident prayer for unity; and for not having become silent so that the Holy Spirit may implant in us the prayer of Jesus on the evening before Good Friday, Lord, have mercy on us.

(Worshipbook, Middle East Council of Churches Assembly, Cyprus, 1990, page 44-45; used by permission of the M.E.C.C.)

Traditional litanies are often used by the older churches of the Middle East and by their weekly repetition become familiar and well-loved prayers. Your group might like to write a new litany using one of the ancient responses such as:

Lord have mercy
O Lord, hear our prayer
From you, O Lord
Kyrie Eleison

Prayer of Intercession

Lord, hear us.

We pray you, O Lord, for our brothers and sisters who are not ashamed to put their trust in your Word even in front of their persecutors.

We pray you, O Lord, for those who are still bound by their past and their dreams and are not yet open to the call of the kingdom which is to come.

We pray you, O Lord, for those who do not dare to hope from you all that you are ready to do for them.

We pray you, O Lord, for all those who, through fear of the necessity of their own transformation, do not dare to hearken to the suffering of their brothers and sister.

(From the Third General Assembly of the Middle East Council of Churches, Cyprus, 1980; used by permission of the M.E.C.C.)

A Prayer from the old Syriac

Used by Christians in Turkey, Iran and South India

To God be glory;
To the angels honor;
To Satan confusion;
To the cross reverence;
To the church exaltation;
To the departed quickening;
To the penitent acceptance;
To the sick and infirm recovery and healing;
And to the four quarters of the world great peace and tranquillity;
And on us who are weak and sinful may the compassion and mercies of our God come, and may they overshadow us continually. Amen.

(Carden, John, compiler, *With All God's People: The New Ecumenical Prayer Cycle*, 1989. Geneva: World Council of Churches, WCC Publications, page 29. Used by permission.)

Prayer

Almighty God, mercifully hear our prayers we offer. Grant us all that is necessary for our spiritual good. Strengthen and confirm the faithful, heal the sick, restore the scornful, uplift the broken. Bless your church; guide its members by your Holy Spirit so that they will do your good will. Grant them faithfulness of heart, and fill us all with zeal so that we will do all for the good of your church and the spread of your kingdom, through Jesus Christ our Lord. Amen.

(Worshipbook, Middle East Council of Churches Assembly, Cyprus, 1990, page 37, used by permission of the M.E.C.C.)

Prayer of Intercession

Lord, hear us.

Awaken in us, O Lord, the desire for the unity of all Christians and convert our hearts.

Purify our faith, removing all merely human interpretations, and make us open to your Word entrusted to your Church.

Teach us, O Lord, to discern the ways which you are now opening up for us to enable your Churches to come together in fellowship.

Make us ready, O Lord, from now on, to do together all the things that our beliefs do not force us to do apart.

(From the Third General Assembly of the Middle East Council of Churches, Cyprus, 1980; used by permission of the M.E.C.C.)

Hymn

Christ Has Called Us to New Visions

Tune: *In Babilone* (8, 7, 8, 7 D)

> Christ has called us to new visions,
> Here to celebrate and praise,
> Here confess our old divisions,
> Here our peace petitions raise.
> Come repentant, come forgiving,
> Come in joy and hope and prayer.
> Christ once crucified now living,
> Bids us faith and love to share.
>
> As we listen to each other,
> As we speak in joy and pain,
> We become as sister, brother,
> Reconciled, at one again.
> Only thus in work and feeling
> For our neighbor far or near
> Can we worship God revealing
> Gifts of grace among us here.
>
> —*Jane Parker Huber*

Huber, Jane Parker, *A Singing Faith*, (Louisville, KY: Westminster/John Knox, 1987), hymn 72. Used by permission of the publisher. Words may be reproduced for one-time group use.

The Scriptures

As Christians one of our ties to the Middle East is its setting for so many events in biblical history. But this very connection can create difficulties. One is the use of the term "Israel," especially in the Psalms, and the possible confusion with the twentieth-century nation-state which bears that same name. It is important to remember that over the centuries Christians have used the term "Israel" to mean "God's people" rather than any geographic entity, and they have interpreted it to include, not exclude, themselves.

A second difficulty is the use of parts of the Old Testament by some people to prove the modern-day Israeli claim to a particular piece of land. This issue, although important to all Christians, takes on a particular poignancy to Palestinian Christians who must live with it on a daily basis. Naim Stifan Ateek, Canon of St. George's Cathedral in Jerusalem, in his book *Justice, and Only Justice: A Palestinian Theology of Liberation*, says that "the *Word* of God incarnate in Jesus the Christ interprets for us the *word* of God in the Bible. To understand God, therefore, the Palestinian Christian, like every other Christian, begins with Christ and goes backward to the Old Testament and forward to the New Testament and beyond them" (page 80). He suggests a simple question to ask in reading and interpreting the Bible: "Does this fit the picture I have of God that Jesus has revealed to me?" (page 82). A fuller discussion of these issues may be found in *Justice and Only Justice: A Palestinian Theology of Liberation*, Maryknoll, NY: Orbis Books, 1989), pages 74-114.

Some Scriptures for use in worship related to this study are:

Psalms 42 and 43—Hope for those in difficult circumstances
Isaiah 2:4 and Micah 4:3-4—Swords into plowshares
Matthew 5:9—Blessed are the peacemakers
Luke 19:41-44—Jesus wept over the city of Jerusalem
Acts 11:19-26—They were first called Christians in Antioch
Romans 14:19—Pursue what makes for peace
Romans 12:1-8—One body, many members
1 Corinthians 12:4-11—Varieties of gifts
2 Corinthians 5:16-21—The ministry of reconciliation
Ephesians 2:13-22—Members of the household of God
Ephesians 4:1-6—One Lord, one faith, one baptism
Hebrews 12:1-2—The great cloud of witnesses
1 Peter 2:4-10—You are like living stones
1 Peter 3:8-12— Seek peace and pursue it

A meditation, homily or sermon might be presented by several people as part of a worship service to share your study with your church. The title could be: "Hard Choices and Hope," focusing on the hard choices that Christians living in the Middle East make, such as how to express their faith in a minority situation and how to serve as peacemakers in violent situations.

Churches of the Middle East

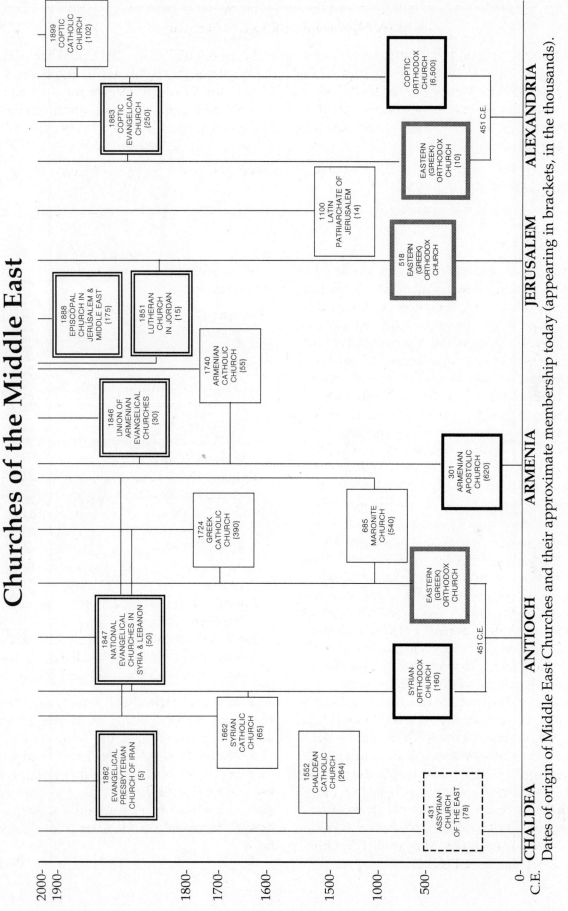

Dates of origin of Middle East Churches and their approximate membership today (appearing in brackets, in the thousands).

ALEXANDRIA

1899 COPTIC CATHOLIC CHURCH [102]

1863 COPTIC EVANGELICAL CHURCH [250]

COPTIC ORTHODOX CHURCH [6,500]

EASTERN (GREEK) ORTHODOX CHURCH [10]

451 C.E.

JERUSALEM

1100 LATIN PATRIARCHATE OF JERUSALEM [14]

518 EASTERN (GREEK) ORTHODOX CHURCH

1888 EPISCOPAL CHURCH IN JERUSALEM & MIDDLE EAST [175]

1851 LUTHERAN CHURCH IN JORDAN [15]

1740 ARMENIAN CATHOLIC CHURCH [55]

1846 UNION OF ARMENIAN EVANGELICAL CHURCHES [30]

ARMENIA

301 ARMENIAN APOSTOLIC CHURCH [620]

ANTIOCH

1724 GREEK CATHOLIC CHURCH [390]

685 MARONITE CHURCH [540]

EASTERN (GREEK) ORTHODOX CHURCH

451 C.E.

1847 NATIONAL EVANGELICAL CHURCHES IN SYRIA & LEBANON [50]

SYRIAN ORTHODOX CHURCH [160]

1662 SYRIAN CATHOLIC CHURCH [65]

CHALDEA

1862 EVANGELICAL PRESBYTERIAN CHURCH OF IRAN [5]

1552 CHALDEAN CATHOLIC CHURCH [264]

431 ASSYRIAN CHURCH OF THE EAST [78]

2000-
1900-
1800-
1700-
1600-
1500-
1000-
500-
0-
C.E.

★

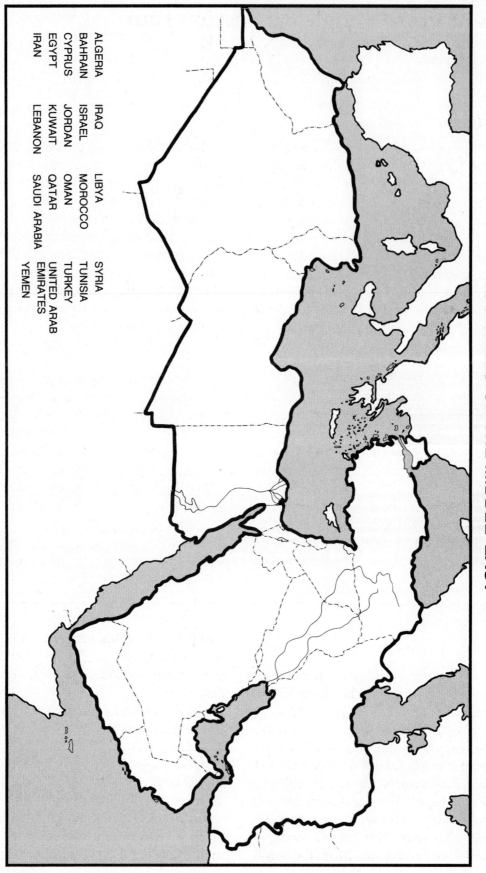

COUNTRIES OF THE MIDDLE EAST

ALGERIA BAHRAIN CYPRUS EGYPT IRAN

IRAQ ISRAEL JORDAN KUWAIT LEBANON

LIBYA MOROCCO OMAN QATAR SAUDI ARABIA

SYRIA TUNISIA TURKEY UNITED ARAB EMIRATES YEMEN

Profiles of Peace People for Session Four

Jeremy Milgrom

Jeremy Milgrom, an American-born rabbi, went to Jerusalem at age 15 to study at a yeshiva for a year. The trip changed his life. He recalls an incredible love for the land and the people but he also remembers a pattern of confrontation. He tells about an incident when he and other yeshiva students closed ranks with their arms around each other, pushing their way through the Old City. He recalls, "I remember seeing terror on some of those faces [of Arab residents] we shoved aside," and he knew that this pattern of behavior on his part was inconsistent with his own values.

Later he was called up into the military for service in the War in Lebanon. Since he believed the war was "unjustly and undemocratically declared," he responded by fasting and eventually being sent home. It was then that he got himself involved with *Yesh G'vul* (There is a Limit). The organization originally supported soldiers who refused to serve in Lebanon and later supported those who refused to do reserve duty on the West Bank. He also has been involved in Peace Now, the largest peace organization in Israel.

Rabbi Milgrom recalls trying to de-escalate a confrontation between Arabs and Jews at Um-el-Fahm, the largest Arab village in Israel. During the incident he was beaten and kicked by the Israeli police. He admits that it is a natural reaction to hit back but he says, ". . . I'm not going to expect that everyone will be a pacifist. I believe in nonviolence because I believe it is always better than violence. People's reactions to violence are infinitely worse than what happens in the violence itself."

Milgrom believes in Zionism as the "communal reconstitution of the Jewish people in Zion," but he does not believe it has to take place at the expense of other people. The kind of Zionism he supports is a progressive kind of Zionism, not to be equated with nationalism. It includes partnership with the Israeli Arabs with whom the Jews share their land. Out of these convictions Jeremy Milgrom continues to work for peace.

A longer piece on Jeremy Milgrom is found in *Unified in Hope: Arabs and Jews Talk About Peace*, from which this profile is taken. See page 60.

Jean Zaru

For five generations, Jean Zaru's family has lived in Ramallah, a town that has been Christian since the late fifteenth century. A Quaker and a Palestinian, Jean remembers experiencing as a child the anguish of the refugees from the 1948 war and how her family of seven shared their three-room apartment for a year with another family. In the 1967 war and occupation it was her own children who were influenced by the situation. She says, "My oldest son was eight, and when we came home [from the bomb shelter] he took his toy guns, and broke all of them with rocks. . . . He said that these things made people suffer, and he didn't want them any more."

Ms. Zaru found herself teaching at the Friends Boys' School out of her own disappointment with the syllabus. Courses in religion and ethics were taught by any teacher who had time in the schedule. When she asked the principal to do more, she was asked to teach herself. Later, when Islam was also taught at the school, she emphasized what the two religions had in common. Now her daughter teaches the courses.

Jean is not only a committed Christian in her personal life but she has also been involved in the local and international YWCA as well as the World Council of Churches. She has participated as a panel member in a number of international gatherings. This has included many dialogues with Jews, especially those who are struggling to change the situation. She realizes, though, that they cannot meet on an equal basis since she is one of the occupied and the Israeli Jews are the occupiers. She affirms her stance as a peacemaker who feels that nonviolence is important, especially in the Middle East. "We do not fight violently because our ultimate goal is a better society for everyone. We want to get rid of evil, not people."

Jean Zaru sees hope in the children and young people and in the fact that her own daughter is committed to live and teach and raise her own child in the midst of the problems on the West Bank. "We cannot live a day without saying yes or no: for death or for life, for war or for peace. But the choice is ours. There is no compromise in this matter. To postpone or evade decision is to decide, to hide the matter is to decide, to compromise is to decide. There is no escape and this is our challenge."

Unified in Hope (see page 60) contains a longer article on Jean Zaru. Material for this profile was also taken from a speech and press release from the 17th General Synod of the United Church of Christ.

Miriam Mar'i

A modern apartment building in Acre, Israel, is a place called home for Dr. Miriam Mar'i, a Muslim and a Palestinian. Dr. Mar'i is an alumna of Haifa University and earned her Ph.D. in international education from the State University of Michigan. She lectures on educational leadership, international education and the status of women in the Arab world, but her principal occupation is as director of Acre's Early Childhood Education Center for the Arab Child. Her own achievements stem from her family's reverence for the principle of education and their intense respect for the study of the Qur'an. Even though she was the youngest of 13 children and a girl, she was sent to school by her family and encouraged to learn by her older sister.

Miriam Mar'i's educational history is remarkable, but it was not all that smooth. Having been taught at home by her older siblings, she encountered misunderstanding and coarse treatment when she first went to the state school. Her teachers, who demanded passivity of their students, denied the possibility that Miriam know anything and made her start all over in learning to read. She is now, in response, dedicating herself to training Arab early-education teachers in the belief that enlightened early education can be used to raise a new generation of curious, self-confident children. She also feels it can help undo the sexual stereotypes the children will encounter later on in their lives.

Although her father was a traditional Muslim who began his prayers each day before dawn, he did not hold a completely traditional understanding of the role of women. Miriam recalls that as a young girl, one of her brothers told her to get him a glass of water. Her father, who was sitting at the head of the table, got up and fetched the water for his son instead, setting it before him silently. "It was my father's way of saying that his son could get his own water." Even though she is frustrated by the narrowmindedness of traditionalism, she believes that the traditional family and community orientation of the Arab people are an important strength and help avoid the alienation seen in the West.

Dr. Mar'i, who identifies herself as a Palestinian Israeli, recognizes that it is complicated to be an Arab citizen of Israel. "I am like a schizophrenic," she says; "I feel the fear on both sides." Even if a Palestinian state were created, she admits she is likely to stay in her home town of Acre. Even so, she longs for that state and a flag of her own.

This profile was compiled from information in the *AJME News*, October-November, 1989 and *New Outlook*.

Profiles of Women for Sessions Five

Nawal el Saadawi

She was dismissed! Dismissed from her job as Egypt's Director of Public Health. Her right to function as editor-in-chief of the magazine *Health* was taken away from her. All of this happened because Nawal el Saadawi's writings on the status of women, particularly her book, *Women and Sex*, were controversial. Saadawi, a medical doctor, writer and feminist was born to an educated family in the rural village of Kafr Tahla in the Delta area of Egypt in the early 1930s. She is proud of her origins and the way in which they have moved her to be concerned for working women of all kinds, from illiterate peasant women to urban women struggling to find jobs.

Dr. Saadawi was heavily involved in peace initiatives at the outset of the Gulf War of 1991. She met with the Secretary General of the U.N. in January and took part in a two-week tour of the United States, hoping to end the war both quickly and with a just peace. The Arab world's struggle for democracy, she believes, will be shelved at this time because of the threat of Western imperialism. This, she sees, is not only a setback for democracy but for women's rights as well.

Active in founding the Arab Women's Solidarity Association, Dr. Saadawi describes her position on Arab women around the theme of "raising the veil from the mind" (the motto of the Association). She takes the position that "by rereading history, Arab women can learn the true reasons why they have been stripped of independence and why male authority was established over them, for these are factors arising from human society, and man-made laws, not from natural or God-given laws" (page 20). She believes that there is no conflict between the authentic Arab personality or identity and modern cultural consciousness. "Being female and Arab is not unlike the human personality of either sex in any society: it is the product of that creativity which links the past with the present, the heritage with current civilization, then goes beyond both history and heritage to a future which is freer, more just and more humane" (page 21).

Dr. Saadawi challenges women to break out of isolation—both in private and public life—and reach out to women of all backgrounds and outlooks. To do so requires political power, which is part of the rationale for the Arab Women's Solidarity Association. She says, "Arab women are on the way, and there is no longer any power on earth than can pull them back" (page 23).

Quotes are from Toubia, Nahid, editor, *Women of the Arab World: The Coming Challenge*. London, Zed Books Ltd., 1988.

Umm Samir and Jamileh

(A composite story in which names have been changed.)

Every morning when the refugee camp in the territories occupied by Israel on the West Bank of the Jordan River is not under curfew or on strike, Umm Samir opens the small grocery store below her house and sells its few goods to the residents of the camp. Because of the troubled economic conditions, she is the main support of her 12-person household. Umm Samir, age 38, is a Palestinian and she lives in a small house with her husband, who is ailing and in his sixties. In addition there are her teen-aged daughter, two step-sons and their wives, her own two school-age sons and three grandchildren. Both the shop and the house are frequently raided by soldiers, and her step-sons are able to find only sporadic employment at minimum wages.

Her sons go to school in the camp and Umm Samir says, "Soldiers harass the children when they leave my door on the way to school and on the way home each day the soldiers are waiting for them. My biggest fear is whether my child will show up at the end of the day." Frequent school closures have also taken a toll on the household and on Umm Samir's nerves. Samir, the oldest (from which Umm Samir gets her name, "mother of Samir"), has been shot with a rubber bullet and the younger son has been beaten.

Umm Samir's daughter, Jamileh, has participated in the clashes and demonstrations in the camp although at first her mother tried to prevent her participation. She remembers that when she first went to demonstrations at the beginning of the *Intifada* (Palestinian uprising) she met groups of young men but did not speak to them because of the social customs. Now she says, "Really, the *shebab's* (young men's) respect for us has increased because of our awareness, and our role in the streets and in the neighborhood committees. We have to give more, make a stronger effort, not to lose this respect and to transfer it to their daily behavior, to reflect the change in the position of women in the future."

Still, Umm Samir worries. "I don't sleep very well any more. I support our Uprising, but women have a very hard role. What is most difficult is the constant fear."

Farida

(The story of Farida is a composite from interviews with a number of Islamic women.)

At age 17 Farida "put *hijab*" (pronounced hee JAHB), as she would term it, which means that she was committed to wear a scarf concealing her hair and neck as well as a long dress covering her arms and legs. "It was a statement of my Islamic religion," she says, "even though my family objected to what I was doing." Farida is now a biologist taking public health courses while her husband studies engineering in the United States. Her home was conservative in customs, she tells us, but not religious in practice. The basis of Islam was taught at home and at school, and she memorized the Qur'an and learned about Islamic law. Nevertheless, embracing the custom of *hijab* was and is a personal decision.

There is a principal concept of Islam, she believes, that there should be separation between males and females. The separation, though, concerns the stranger, not men in the family. Fathers, brothers and uncles are men you cannot marry, so you can take off *hijab* in front of them. Farida tells us that she wears make-up and beautiful dresses at home with her husband or on occasions with only women present, but when she goes out in public she takes off the make-up and puts on her scarf and long dress.

When asked about how the separation would affect other activities, Farida describes being uncomfortable in a mixed high school gym class, so she withdrew and did sports at home. Mixed swimming pools are inconceivable to her, and even in medical care, she believes that women doctors should examine women and men doctors care for men. If there is an emergency or only one specialist, there could be an exception but separation would be the norm. If she were a doctor she would share in operating with a man but definitely would want her sterilized clothing to include a long skirt and head scarf rather than Western operating room clothing.

What are the advantages of *hijab* to women? Farida tells us that the *hijab* is a preventative. It would prevent the kind of life where there are teen-age pregnancies, sexual diseases, rape and adultery. Men and women would both be more comfortable by being with their own kind. She cites the example of the all-female class for teenagers she teaches at the Mosque. In it the young women take off their scarves, feel at ease, and feel free to ask more questions. Where there is this separation, women would be respected as persons of dignity rather than looked at as sex objects. Their skills and achievements would be taken seriously. Since knowledge is important to Islam, Farida believes that the education of women would increase in an Islamic society.

Farida is clear that moving from a colonial and Westernized society to a more Islamic society is what she is working for in her life. She says, "Islam is a culture. The environment says it's Islam. The way you treat your neighbors; the way the family helps each other says it's Islam. The way you dress outside the home says its Islam."

Maud Nahas

It was the Orthodox youth movement of the 1960s that brought Maud Nahas into a leadership position in the church. It was the same youth movement that trained many of today's Middle Eastern church leaders and that brought creativity and renewal into the church through Bible studies, weekly group meetings, liturgical renewal and social work. Today, no longer a youth, Maud works for the Orthodox Archdiocese of Mt. Lebanon (part of the Greek Orthodox Patriarchate of Antioch and All the East) in suburban Beirut. She was trained in psychology and pedagogy and worked twelve years as a teacher before she decided to dedicate her life to the church, especially in Christian education.

Maud's present work involves coordinating the social aspects of pastoral care both for the archdiocese and in local parishes. During the fighting in Beirut in the late 1970s and 1980s, Maud and a number of other women continued to move throughout the city and countryside, crossing the green line daily and constantly exposing themselves to danger. She tells stories of children losing months of school and needing to be tutored and of people spending enormous energy on acquiring just the necessities of life. Everything takes three times as long and no one has time for extras, she explains. When they turn to the church, they are afraid and it is the church that tries to turn their fear into faith.

A co-worker of Maud's, speaking at the Sixth Assembly of the World Council of Churches, described the situation in Lebanon as: "The experience of death in the midst of life. A whole nation living under the sign of the cross, a country living under death, living in this constant boundary situation between death and life, reaching out with Thomas and feeling the sting of death in an immediate first-hand touch of the risen Christ, and thus tasting the sweetness and glory of life confronting and overcoming death. . . . And as one goes through the purifying fire of boundary situations, all that is non-essential disappears." It is in this situation that Maud lives and works.

When asked whether she as a woman encounters any obstacles to working in the Orthodox Church, Maud replies, "You don't wait to be asked. You feel responsible for the Church and you do it. Of course you have difficulties, so you overcome them." In the eyes of the people who know her, she is the woman in Beirut "who distributes Gospels and blankets."

This profile is written from interviews with Maud and other people. The quote by her co-worker is from "Sixth Assembly: A Missionary Perspective," in *International Review of Mission*, Vol. LXXII, No. 288, Oct 1983, p. 512. Copyright, World Council of Churches, WCC Publications.

Folktales

The Thousand and One Nights (*Alf Laylah wa Laylah*) is probably the Arabic work most familiar to Westerners. Indeed, it may be the only work of Arabic literature known to some. Yet Middle Eastern literature, both from various historic periods and from the many cultural groups within the Middle East, is much richer in form and content. Translation, of course, has been one problem, but simple unfamiliarity with customs and ideas as well as a single-minded focus on Western literature in our educational systems has left this area quite unexplored by most Westerners.

Of all the forms of literature, the most accessible is the folktale, of which The Thousand and One Nights is considered to be a collection of inferior quality. One of the most popular collections is *Kalila wa Dimna*, tales read by every school child, in which wit, courage and moral advice are shown in interactions of animals.

The circle of men drinking coffee and smoking in a coffee house or public bath while listening to a storyteller and the roomful of women listening to a wise elder illustrating sensitive women's issues with stories are no longer ordinary daily activities in the Middle East. Television, as in our countries, has taken over the place of storytelling, but here and there people are preserving this most ancient of traditions.

Included here are several stories that can be used in adult study groups as well as in programs for children or youth.

The Cat Who Went to Mecca

This tale from Syria speaks of the Hajj, or trip to Mecca, which all good Muslims are expected to take one time in their lives. There is an expectation that on return the pilgrim is a new person in behavior and in devotion.

A long time ago the king of the cats went on the pilgrimage to Mecca. When he returned, the king of the mice felt obligated to pay him the traditional visit of congratulations on his safe return as a Hajji, or pilgrim. He said to his subjects the mice, "Etiquette demands that we go to his house and welcome him back formally." The mice were not convinced. "The cat is our enemy; how can we go near him in safety?" The king explained, "Now that he has been to Mecca and become a Hajji, he is no longer free to do what was permitted before. Nowadays he remains at prayer from dawn till sunset, and the prayer beads never leave his hands." The mice were not persuaded. "You call on him and see," they said. "We shall wait here for you."

So the king of the mice set out. He poked his head out of his hole and looked around. There sat the king of the cats, the white cap of a pilgrim on his head. He was praising God, murmuring prayers, and every now and then spitting over his shoulder, first to his left and then to his right, in case the devil was lurking behind to distract him from his devotions.

But no sooner had the king of the cats caught sight of the king of the mice peeping out of his hole than he dropped his rosary and sprang! And but for God the Preserver, he would have bitten the mouse's tail right off.

The king of the mice jumped back into his hole and rejoined his subjects. "How is the king of the cats after his pilgrimage?" they asked. "Let's hope he has changed for the better." "Never mind the pilgrimage," said the king of the mice. "He may pray like a Hajji, but he still pounces like a cat."

The Emir of Bedouins and His Guarantee

This story illustrates some of the customs of hospitality among the Bedouin as well as behavior that would be considered trustworthy among such people.

In the Nadj area of the Arabian Peninsula, there was a season of drought—no rain, consequently, no crops. The Emir of a bedouin tribe was renowned for his generosity, especially towards his tribes-people in helping the needy when necessary. So his people came to him asking for help because they were almost starving. But he told them: "My dear friends, I am myself in the same case as you, and if any one of you can give me counsel which is possible for me to fulfill, I am ready to do the same."

So they told him: "In Hooran (Syria) there is a village where several people have cisterns full of wheat. Surely through your fame, if you ask them to lend you the necessary wheat to be repaid next crop, they will not refuse your request." So they prepared themselves and, with a number of bedouin notables, went to try, if possible, to get the wanted wheat. When they arrived at the village, they were welcomed by the Sheikh of the village, and his servants took care of their horses while others spread the carpets and invited the bedouins to sit down. Immediately, coffee was prepared and tobacco offered and conversation went on. Immediately, as well, a sheep was slaughtered and rice was prepared. When the lunch meal was ready, the servants arrived with their jugs to enable the guests to wash their hands, and when the lunch was over again water was brought with soap to enable the guests to wash their hands and mouths.

Then the Emir said to his host: "May God and the Prophet recompense you." The Sheikh said in answer: "May the food give you health and strength." When the coffee was offered and the pipes were filled with tobacco, the village people, as is their custom, started to compete among themselves in a regular make-believe dispute as to who would prepare supper for the guest; one would say: "I will do the supper," and another would swear that he would do the supper and so on till the Sheikh or one of the elders of the village used his right to assign the man who would do the supper.

Then the Sheikh asked the Emir about the purpose of the happy visit and the Emir answered: "We come to ask you to sell us wheat on credit for the next crop when all shall be paid, with our thanks for your help." The Sheikh then ordered his servants to fill the sacks and made the accounts and asked the Emir for a guarantee of payment. Then the Emir took out his comb and combed his beard. Three hairs were left in the comb, so the Emir took them, wrapped them up in a piece of paper. He then gave them to the Sheikh saying to him: "Keep these hairs as a guarantee till I pay you; they are from my beard and therefore they are of great value." The Sheikh ordered his men to help the bedouins load the sacks on their camels, took the folded hairs, kissed them and put them on his head, a gesture which meant acceptance and respect. The bedouins then departed content with the bargain of their Emir.

In the neighborhood near their tribe, there was another Emir, but renowned for his avarice and stinginess. When he heard about the success of his neighbor in getting wheat on credit for which he placed three hairs of his beard as guarantee, he went also to do the same. After arriving at the same village and after food was served, he asked the Sheikh of the village to give him wheat as he did to his neighbor. So the Sheikh had the sacks filled with wheat, calculated the price and asked for a guarantee. The Emir told him: "My neighbor gave you three hairs of his beard as a guarantee, I will give you a lot." He then tore the hair of his beard and offered it to the Sheikh. But the Sheikh did not accept it and ordered his men to take the wheat back, saying to the Emir: "If you give away the hairs of your beard so easily and in a large number, this is a sure indication that you do not consider them valuable, which means you will not keep your word concerning repayment of your debt."

From *Arab Folktales from Artas*, edited by Abdullatif M. Barghouti, Birzeit University, 1987, pages 183-185. Used by permission.

Si'Djeha and the Qadi's Coat

Si'Djeha, pronounced see-deh-RAH, of North Africa is variously known as Djuha, Djawha, Djahan, or Giufa' in the Medditeranean and Middle East area. Closely related, if not the same, is the character Mullah Nasrudin or Khodja Nassreddin, who appears in folk tales from Turkey to Iran, and even beyond to India and Pakistan. He is sometimes a trickster and sometimes a wise fool, but he is always clever and wins in the end. A Qadi (pronounced KAH-dee) in this story from Tunisia is a judge of an Islamic court of justice. It is important to remember that Islam forbids the drinking of alcohol.

One day Si'Djeha was strolling on the outskirts of the town when he came upon the Qadi snoring under a tree, working off his last wine-drinking bout. So deeply sunk in sleep was the judge that Si'Djeha was able to pull his fine woolen cloak off him without making him stir.

When the Qadi woke up and saw that he had been robbed of his costly coat, he sent his men to search for it. They soon recognized it on Si'Djeha's back and dragged him to court. "How did you come to possess so fine a cloak?" demanded the Qadi. "I saw it on an unbeliever grossly drunk with the stink of wine upon him lying asleep under a tree. So I spit on his infidel beard and took his coat. But if your honor claims the cloak, it is only just that you should have it back." "I have never seen this coat before in my life," hissed the Qadi. "Now be off with you, and take the coat along too."

The Smuggler

This story features Nasrudin but the tale is familiar even in the West. What are some other ways you have heard it told?

Time and again Nasrudin passed from Persia to Greece on donkey-back. Each time he had two panniers of straw, and trudged back without them. Every time the guard searched him for contraband. They never found any.

"What are you carrying, Nasrudin?"

"I am a smuggler."

Years later, more and more prosperous in appearance, Nasrudin moved to Egypt. One of the customs men met him there.

"Tell me, Mulla, now that you are out of the jurisdiction of Greece and Persia, living here in such luxury—what was it that you were smuggling when we could never catch you?"

"Donkeys."

The Talking Turkeys

Just as everyone enjoys the tale of a wise fool, women in particular enjoy stories of wily women who outwit men. In a culture that often restricts women, such tales are even more delicious. This tale is from Syria and the outwitting is done in a very round-about way.

Once when the sultan was sick, he did not leave the palace for thirty days. Finally he recovered and felt well enough to step out. Now it happened that a sly old woman saw him and hurried into the women's reception hall to congratulate the queen on her husband's regained health.

As she was sitting in the queen's presence, the old woman noticed that there were about a hundred turkeys in the courtyard outside the window. So she said to the sultan's wife, "O Queen of our time, can these birds of yours talk?" Naturally, the queen said "No." "If you let me have them for sixty nights, I'll teach them to speak in seven tongues," said the old woman. The queen agreed to have the birds trained.

"But," said the old woman, "I shall need provisions to feed them. One hundred sacks of flour, one measure of nuts, one measure of sugar, and so much of this and so much of that." The queen agreed. She gave the order, and they brought what the old woman had asked for.

When the sixty days were almost past, the old woman went to the queen looking very distressed. She said, "These birds of yours are saying strange things, and much as I beat them they will not change their song." "What are they saying?" asked the queen. "They say: 'Tsk! Tsk! The sultan's daughter has a lover!'" said the old woman. The queen now looked distressed. "Kill them at once," She said. "And whatever you do, don't bring them back to the palace."

The old woman obeyed the queen. She kept the turkeys in her house, dining on them herself and cooking some of them for her son's wedding feast.

A Party for Coats

This story is adapted from a Turkish folktale. It has its parallel in James 2:1-5.

"You must hurry," friends cried to the Teacher as he rushed home from the fields. "The banquet at the home of Halil has alrady begun. You are late."

They are right, the Teacher thought. If I take the time to change clothes, I could miss the entire dinner. Instead of returning to his home he proceeded in his work clothes to the home of Halil, the rich man.

When he arrived the servants at the door refused to allow him to enter because he was not dressed properly. Though he protested, the servants stood firm.

Finally, the Teacher walked to the home of a friend who lived nearby. He borrowed a nice coat and quickly returned to the party. He was immediately welcomed and was seated at the banquet table.

When the food was served, the Teacher began to put it on his coat. He smeared his jacket with vegetables and poured the appetizer in his pocket. All the time he said loudly, "Eat, dear dinner jacket. I hope you are enjoying the meal."

All the guests focused their attention on the Teacher's strange behavior. Finally, Halil asked, "Why are you telling your jacket to enjoy the meal?"

"When I arrived in my work clothes," the Teacher explained, "I was refused entrance. It was only when I was accompanied by this fine coat that I was allowed to sit at the table. Naturally I assume that it was the jacket, not me, that was invited to your banquet."

Proverbs

Middle Easterners make abundant use of proverbs, of which they have hundreds. Wisdom and insight are demonstrated by a person's knowledge of proverbs, and a person's image is enhanced by their proper use. See if you can think of Western proverbs that express the same idea as these Middle Eastern proverbs.

The world is changeable, one day honey and the next day onions.

If a rich man ate a snake, they would say it was because of his wisdom; if a poor man ate it, they would say it was because of his stupidity.

Patience is beautiful.

The eye cannot rise above the eyebrow.
  (Be satisfied with your station in life.)

Your tongue is like a horse—if you take care of it, it takes care of you; if you treat it badly, it treats you badly.

The dogs may bark but the caravan moves on.
  (A person should rise above petty criticism.)

The monkey in the eyes of its mother is a gazelle.

Above proverbs from Nydell, Margaret K. 1987. *Understanding Arabs: A Guide for Westerners* (Yarmouth, Maine: Intercultural Press Inc., 1987), pages 108-109. Used with permission.

Be not proud because you are learned, but discourse with the ignorant as with the sage.

Wisdom is in the head and not in the notebook.

Learning is a treasury whose keys are questions.

Come now and give me a hand; I will do the same for you one day.

Paradise without people is not worth setting foot in.

Propose marriage through your ears, not through your eyes.
  (Set more store by a person's reputation than looks.)

I hear noise but see no grinding.

One hand does not clap.

Don't cut the tree that shades you.

If you see a lion's teeth, don't mistake it for a smile.

These proverbs from Shabbas, Audrey, and Al-Qazzaz, Ayad, editors, *Arab World Notebook* (Berkeley, Calif.: Najda: Women Concerned About the Middle East, 1989), pages 117–120. Reprinted by permission.

★

Middle Eastern Food

Great value is attached to food and the preparation of food in the Middle East. In that world of strong family ties, large clans and women at home, hospitality and gregariousness are deeply entrenched; offering food is the central act in the highly developed art of pleasing.

The style of preparing food, the proportion of ingredients and the particular spices used are different in every town, every village and indeed in every family. They are as varied as the Middle East itself. There are rural foods and urban ones, foods that belong to the desert, others that belong to the mountain, the plain or the seacoast, nomadic foods and street foods. Since a great deal of cooking uses fresh food, there are also many seasonal variations. Many general characteristics are, nonetheless, shared by food preparation in all the countries.

Middle Eastern cooking is a very sensual kind of cooking, using herbs, spices, and aromatics generously. Certain methods, like skewer cooking over charcoal or long, slow simmering in unglazed covered pots, are typical of the whole region. All the countries have rice and wheat dishes, stuffed vegetables, pies wrapped in paper-thin pastry, meatballs, thick omelettes, cold vegetables cooked in oil, scented rice puddings, nut-filled pastries, fritters soaked in syrup and many other elements in common. You find raisins with pine nuts everywhere, garnishes of chopped pistachios and almonds, and the same food combinations, such as chickpeas with spinach.

Adapted from "Middle Eastern Cooking: The Legacy" by Claudia Roden, *Aramco World*, March-April, 1988. Used by permission.

Appetizers are an important introduction to a meal. They may include dips, pickles of all types, olives, cheeses and fresh vegetables. Soups of many kinds, including lentil, chicken, and mixed vegetable, are enjoyed. For a main course several dishes are served. Stuffed vegetables are popular as are stuffed grape leaves. Meat and vegetable stews with rice or other grains as well as roast chicken, meat or fish may be served. Dessert is likely to be some fresh fruit, although for special occasions, sweets and pastries might be served. When all is done, strong, sweet coffee or perhaps mint tea or even both complete the meal.

Hospitality is a duty and a pleasure throughout the Middle East. Often great numbers of dishes are placed on the table for the guest. The traditional dining table may actually be a large metal tray resting on wooden legs. If so, the diners will sit around the table on cushions. In Arab homes the word *"Bismillah"* ("In the name of God") is said by everyone before eating.

The recipes below include some relatively simple dishes that can be prepared with ingredients from the supermarket. Health food stores may also sell some of the ingredients, or you can write one of these mail order companies:

G. B. Ratto & Company
(broad variety of spices and foods)
821 Washington Street
Oakland, CA 94607
1-800-325-3483
FAX: 415-836-2250

Shatila Foods
(bakery goods)
8505 W. Warren
Dearborn, MI 48126
1-313-934-1520
FAX: 313-934-3232

Sultan's Delight, Inc.
(broad variety of spices and foods)
P.O. Box 153
Staten Island NY 10314
1-800-852-5046

Mjedarra

Mjedarra (pronounced mm-JED-dah-rah) is known as a dish of the poor people but it is a popular favorite in the Middle East. The proportions of ingredients vary. This version is a family recipe from Jordan.

> 2 cups lentils
> 1 cup long grain rice
> 1 large onion finely chopped
> 3/4 cup olive oil
> 1 Tbsp salt (or more to taste)

Cook lentils in 6 cups of water for about 15 minutes. Add rice and cook another 20 minutes. Heat olive oil in pan and saute chopped onion in oil. Mix onion and oil into lentil/rice mixture. Add salt to taste. Serve or set aside in the refrigerator and heat over low flame or in microwave oven when ready to serve. This dish is good fresh or as a leftover. The lentils should stay whole in this dish. If they are mushy, try cooking it a little less next time. Serve with a dab of yogurt.

Hummus bi Tahini

The following proportions are approximate because every family has its own way of preparing this dip. Raw garbanzo beans, soaked and cooked, may be used instead of canned.

> 2 cans pre-cooked garbanzo beans (also
>   known as chickpeas)
> 2 cloves garlic
> juice of one lemon
> 1 Tbsp olive oil
> 1/4 to 1/2 cup tahini (sesame seed paste,
>   available in large supermarkets, health
>   food stores or by mail order)

Mash the garbanzo beans until they make a smooth paste. Crush the garlic and add it along with the oil, lemon juice, and tahini. Blend well, adding more of any ingredient to taste. A food processor, blender or mixer are all helpful tools for making this dish, although it can be made by hand. Serve as a dip with pita bread broken into small pieces. Try toasting the pieces of pita in the oven first.

Lebneh

Lebneh is simply yogurt with the excess water drained out.

> 1 quart of plain yogurt (may be low fat, if
>   desired).

Line a colander with two layers of paper towels or a layer of unbleached muslin. Pour in yogurt. Put plastic wrap on top and a saucer or small plate on top of that. (The plate should be small enough to go further down in the colander as the bulk is diminished.) Put a one pound weight, such as a can of tomato sauce, on top of the plate. Place the colander in a pan or leave in the sink overnight to catch the water draining off. In the morning the lebneh is ready to use as a spread or a dip. It will be the consistency of soft cream cheese and needs refrigera-tion if not used immediately. It can be used as is or in one of the variations below.

1. Add finely chopped cucumbers and black olives. Dry mint is another variation. Serve with pieces of pita bread.

2. Put into a flat dish or bowl and make a hollow indentation in center. Pour olive oil into hollow. Again offer pieces of pita bread for scooping up portions.

3. Spread lebneh on wedges of pita bread or toasted English muffins and sprinkle with a mixture of spices. (Any combination of marjoram, oregano or basil as well as toasted sesame seeds make a nice mixture.)

4. Mold the lebneh into balls, dip into olive oil and sprinkle with paprika.

Baklava Rolls

adapted from several recipes and several friends

> 1 package filo dough (available in the frozen dessert section of supermarkets or by mail order)
> 1 pound melted butter (Splurge and use butter.)
> 4 cups ground English walnuts
> 1/2 cup sugar

Cook up syrup using either of the two recipes below. Cool. Mix together nuts, sugar and 2 Tablespoons melted butter. Set aside. Butter a baking tray and preheat the oven to 325 degrees.

As you use the sheets of filo dough, keep the pile of unused sheets covered with plastic wrap and a damp dish towel. As you work, lift the sheets carefully by hand and recover the pile immediately. Place the sheets of dough on the counter one at a time and brush with melted butter until you have a pile of 4 or 5 sheets. Spread 3/4 cup of the nut mixture along the long side of the stack of sheets and then roll it up. Place on a baking tray. Make angled cuts partway through the rolled dough every inch or so. Brush the roll with melted butter and bake about 20 to 40 minutes, according to your oven, or until slightly brown. Remove from oven and pour cold syrup over the hot roll. Let cool and cut all the way through.

Syrup #1

> 1 cup honey
> 1 1/2 cup sugar
> 1 1/4 cup water
> juice of one lemon

Mix ingredients together, cooking ten minutes at a low boil and then set aside to cool completely before pouring over hot dessert. The syrup will be quite thin.

Syrup #2

> 2 cups sugar
> 1 cup water
> 3 drops lemon juice
> 1 teaspoon rose water or orange blossom water

Combine first three ingredients and boil for 15 minutes. Add rose water or orange blossom water and let cool completely before pouring over hot dessert.

Two helpful cookbooks are:
Food from Biblical Lands by Helen Corey, available from Americans for Middle East Understanding, Inc. (address on page 53).
A Book of Middle Eastern Food by Claudia Roden, available from American Educational Trust (address on page 53).

★

Names in Arab Cultures

In many Western societies, one indication of the closeness of a personal relationship is the use of first names. In Arab society, the first name is used immediately, even if it is preceded by "Miss," "Mrs." or "Mr."

Arabs do not refer to people by the "last" name. Arab names, for both men and women, comprise a first name (the person's own), their father's name, and their paternal grandfather's name, followed by a family name (in countries where family names are used). In other words, an Arab's name is a list of ancestors on the father's side. It would be the same as if a Westerner's name were John (given name) Robert (his father) William (his grandfather) Jones.

Because names reflect genealogy on the father's side, women have masculine names after their first name. Some people include "ibn" (son of) or "bint" (daughter of) between the ancestral names. This practice is common in the Arabian Peninsula; for example, Abdel-Aziz ibn Saud (son of Saud), the founder of the Kingdom of Saudi Arabia. In North Africa the word "ben" or "ould" is used to mean "son of." "Bou," which means "father of," is also a common element of a family name. Examples are Chadli Bendjedid, President of Algeria, Mohamed Khouna Ould Haidalla, President of Mauritania, and Habib Bourguiba, former President of Tunisia.

Because a person's first name is the only one which is really his or hers, Arabs use it from the moment they are introduced. A Western man can expect to be called "Mr. Bill" or "Mr. John." If he is married, his wife will be called "Mrs. Mary," or possibly "Mrs. Bill." First names are also used with titles, such as "Doctor" and "Professor."

A person may retain several names for legal purposes but often omit them in daily use. A man named Ahmad Abdallah Ali Mohammed would be commonly known as Ahmad Abdallah; if he has a family or tribal name such as Al-Harithi, he would be known as Admad Abdallah Al-Harithi, or possibly Ahmad Al-Harithi. People are not always consistent when reciting their names on different occasions. In some Arab countries, the telephone book even lists people under their first names, because the first name is the only one which can be depended upon to be consistently present.

An Arab woman does not [necessarily] change her name after marriage, since she cannot take her husband's genealogy, which is what it would imply. Besides, Arabs are very proud of their mother's family and want her to retain the name and refer to it. Only informally is a wife called "Mrs." with her husband's first or last name.

When people have children, an informal but very polite way to address them is "father of" (abu) or "mother of" (umm) the oldest son or oldest child, as in Umm Ahmad, "mother of Ahmad."

Arabs do not name their sons after the father, but naming a child after his paternal grandfather is common. You will meet many men whose first and third names are the same.

Here are a few simple guidelines.

1. If a name sounds Western (George, William, Mary), it marks a Christian.

2. If a name is that of a well-known figure in Islamic history (Mohammad, Bilal, Salah-Eddeen, Fatima, Ayesha), it marks a Muslim.

3. Most hyphenated names using "Abdel-" are Muslim. The name means "Servant (Slave) of God," and the second part is one of the attributes of God (Abdallah, "Servant of Allah"; Abdel-Rahman, "Servant of the Merciful"; Abdel-Karim, "Servant of the Generous"). There are a

few Christian names on this pattern (Abdel-Malak, "Servant of the Angel"; Abdel-Massih, "Servant of the Messiah"), but over 90 per cent of the time you can assume that a person with this type of name is Muslim. Muslims list 99 attributes for God altogether (All-Powerful, All-Knowing, Compassionate, All-Wise, etc.), and most of these are presently in use as names.

4. Names containing the word "Deen" (religion) are Muslim (Sharaf-Eddeen, "The Honor of Religion"; Badr-Eddeen, "The Moon of Religion"; Sayf-Eddeen, "The Sword of Religion").

5. Most Arab names have a meaning, so many are simply descriptive adjectives (Aziz, "dear"; Said, "happy"; Amin, "faithful"; Hasan, "good"). Such descriptive names do not mark religion.

6. Names that are both Qur'anic and Biblical (Ibrahim, "Abraham"; Sulaiman, "Solomon"; Daoud, "David"; Yousef, "Joseph") do not mark religion.

From Nydell, Margaret K., 1987. *Understanding Arabs: A Guide for Westerners*. Yarmouth, Maine: Intercultural Press, Inc. Used with permission.

★

Words, words, words

It is never quite possible to convey the pronunciation of words in another language when writing in English. There are sounds that are unfamiliar and some that seem to be "between" two English sounds. So, if you can get a native speaker to pronouce these words, do so. Syllables in capital letters are accented.

In Arabic

Hello—MAR ha bah

Good morning—sa BAH el khair (response: sa BAH el nur)

Good evening—mas SA el khair (response: mas SA el nur)

Thank you—show KRAN

You're welcome—af WAN

God willing—in SHA lah

Peace—sa LA am

Peace be with you—sa LA am el EYE koom No-LAH

Yes—EYE wah

In Turkish

Hello—hosh GEL dinez

Good morning—goon EYE den

Good evening—EE ak SHAM lar

Thank you—tesh EE ker AH der im

You're welcome—bir SHAY DE hil

Peace—SUHL

In Hebrew

Good morning—BO ker TOVH

Good evening—LAY lah to VAH

Thank you—to DAH

You're welcome—be VAH keh SHAH

Peace—sha LOHM

Hello—sha LOHM

Goodbye—sha LOHM

In Persian

(aa represents the sound of "a" as in "sap")

Hello—saa LAHM

Good morning—SOHBH bekh AYR

Good evening—AASR bekh AYR

Good night—SHAAB bekh AYRE

Good-bye (God be your keeper)—kho DA ha FEZ

Thank you—moh teh SHACK KER am

You are welcome—KHOSH ahm maah DEED

To greet people in other Middle Eastern languages:

The following greetings are from Soghikian, Juanita Will, Lands, Peoples and Communities of the Middle East (Fountain Hills, Arizona: Middle East Gateway Series, 1991), page 1.

In Berber - sa LAAM a la KUM

In Armenian - pa REE yeh GAR

In Kurdish - bih khayr HAA tii

Addresses for Further Resources

Since most Christians in the Middle East are of Arab background, the following sources of information about issues will be most useful to understand their viewpoint. Information from these sources is more likely to be slanted toward the Arab side of Middle East conflicts:

AMERICAN-ARAB ANTI-DISCRIMINATION COMMITTEE
4201 Connecticut Ave. N.W., Suite 500
Washington, DC 20008   (202) 797-7662
This organization strives to counteract poor images of Arabs in the media along with working to prevent anti-Arabism.

AMERICAN EDUCATIONAL TRUST
P.O. Box 53062
Washington, DC 20009   (800) 368-5788
Publishes "The Washington Report on Middle East Affairs" monthly. Source of books at a discount.

AMERICANS FOR MIDDLE EAST UNDER-STANDING
475 Riverside Dr.
New York, NY 10115   (212) 870-2053
Publishes "The Link," a newsletter for churches; each issue focuses on a different subject. Recent issues have included the post-war Middle East and reviews of books on the Middle East. Also a source of books at a discount.

AMIDEAST
110 17th St. NW
Washington, DC 20036   (202) 785-0022
Publishes the *Arab World Almanac* available to secondary school teachers.

Canadian Arab Federation
5298 Dundas St., West
Etobicoke, Ontario M9B 1B2   (416) 231-7524
A national organization made up of local groups; publishes the *Arab Canadian* and works to inform Canadian public about the Arab world.

MIDDLE EAST RESEARCH AND INFORMA-TION PROJECT (MERIP)
1500 Massachusetts Ave., N.W.
Washington, DC 20005   (202) 223-3677

Publishes "Middle East Report," six times a year. Often issues have special focus, such as oil, arms, roles of women, etc. Also compiles special resource packets and short, useful "primers" on certain issues.

NAJDA: WOMEN CONCERNED ABOUT THE MIDDLE EAST
P.O. Box 7152
Berkeley, CA 94707   (415) 549-3512
Publishes resources for children, youth, and adults.

For a Jewish point of view on the Middle East:

AMERICAN JEWISH COMMITTEE
165 East 56th Street
New York, NY 10022   (212) 751-4000

ANTI-DEFAMATION LEAGUE OF B'NAI B'RITH
823 United Nations Plaza
New York, NY 10017   (212) 490-2525

Ecumenical organizations for Middle East education and advocacy:

MIDDLE EAST PROGRAMS, AFSC
See denominational offices section,
American Friends Service Committee

MIDDLE EAST COMMITTEE
Canadian Council of Churches
40 St. Clair Avenue East
Toronto, Ontario M4T 1M9   (416) 921-4152

CHURCHES FOR MIDDLE EAST PEACE
110 Maryland Ave., NE, Suite 108
Washington, DC 20202   (202) 546-8425
An advocacy group for some 20 communions and church-related organizations. See *Angle of Vision*, pages 110-111.

MIDDLE EAST COUNCIL OF CHURCHES
P.O. Box 4259
Limassol, Cyprus

MIDDLE EAST PEACE MAKERS
P.O. Box 836
Teaneck, NJ 07666   (201) 833-0525

★

Middle East Peace Makers *(continued)*
A network for support and resources for several denominations. See *Angle of Vision*, page 110.

MIDDLE EAST OFFICE
National Council of Churches
475 Riverside Drive, Room 614
New York, NY 10115   (212) 870-2811

U.S. INTERRELIGIOUS COMMITTEE FOR
PEACE IN THE MIDDLE EAST
Greene & Westview, 3rd Floor
Philadelphia, PA 19119   (215) 438-4142
Brings together Jews, Christians and Muslims who agree on need for negotiated settlement of Israeli/Palestinian conflict. See *Angle of Vision*, page 116.

Addresses of denominational offices

AFRICAN METHODIST EPISCOPAL
CHURCH
P.O. Box 183
St. Louis, MO 63166

AMERICAN BAPTIST CHURCHES
P.O. Box 851
Valley Forge, PA 19181

AMERICAN FRIENDS SERVICE COMMITTEE
1501 Cherry Street
Philadelphia, PA 19102 (215) 241-7142

ARMENIAN MISSIONARY ASSOCIATION
140 Forrest Avenue
Paramus, NJ 07652

CHRISTIAN CHURCH (DISCIPLES OF
CHRIST)
Division of Overseas Ministries
P.O. Box 1986
Indianapolis, IN 46206

CHURCH OF THE BRETHREN
1451 Dundee Avenue
Elgin, IL 60120-1694

CHURCH OF GOD
P.O. Box 2338
Anderson, IN 46018

EPISCOPAL CHURCH CENTER
815 Second Avenue
New York, NY 10017

EVANGELICAL LUTHERAN CHURCH IN
AMERICA
8765 W. Higgins Road
Chicago, IL 60631

FRIENDS UNITED MEETING
245 Second Street, NE
Washington, DC 20002

MENNONITE BOARD OF MISSIONS
Box 370
Elkhart IN 46515

MENNONITE CENTRAL COMMITTEE
21 South 12th Street
Akron, PA 17501

PRESBYTERIAN CHURCH IN CANADA
50 Wynford Drive
Don Mills, Ontario M3C 1J7

PRESBYTERIAN CHURCH (USA)
100 Witherspoon Street
Louisville, KY 40402-1396

REFORMED CHURCH IN AMERICA
Room 1826, 475 Riverside Drive
New York, NY 10115

SEVENTH DAY ADVENTIST
12501 Old Colunbia Pike
Silver Springs, MD 20904

SOUTHERN BAPTIST FOREIGN MISSION
BOARD
P.O. Box 6767
Richmond, VA 23230

UNITED CHURCH OF CANADA
85 St. Clair Ave. East
Toronto, Ontario M4T 1M8

UNITED CHURCH OF CHRIST BOARD FOR
WORLD MINISTRIES
700 Prospect Ave.
Cleveland, OH 44115

UNITED METHODIST CHURCH, WORLD
DIVISION
Room 1550, 475 Riverside Drive
New York, NY 10115

Bibliography

This Bibliography offers a select sampling from the multitude of books on the Middle East. The Annotated Bibliography in *Angle of Vision* by Charles Kimball includes a list of the basic books on the Middle East; leaders should begin there for resources. The following list includes some of the books mentioned in this study guide plus many others, and does not duplicate the *Angle of Vision* list.

Look for these and other resources in church libraries, local public and college libraries, bookstores, and denominational resource centers. Prices and availabilty of books may change. Books and resources from Friendship Press to complement the Middle East study are listed on the inside back cover and on page 60. Please do *not* order books of other publishers as listed in this bibliography from Friendship Press.

The author and editor are grateful to Mary Beth Courdo and Charles Kimball for assistance with this listing.

Overviews of the Middle East

Carter, Jimmy. *The Blood of Abraham: Insights Into the Middle East.* Boston: Houghton Mifflin, 1986. $7.95 paper. The former president demystifies each nation's history, political expectations, prime concerns and differing goals. He offers a reconciling vision for all—Jews, Moslems and Christians.

Congressional Quarterly editors. *The Middle East, Seventh Edition Revised.* Washington, D.C.: Congressional Quarterly, Inc., 1991. $24.95, oversize paper. Huge and informative, provides overview and background on conflicts in region, politics, economics, plus extensive profiles of countries and regions, detailed chronology 1900-1989, bibliography.

Glass, Charles. *Tribes with Flags: A Dangerous Passage Through the Chaos of the Middle East.* New York: Atlantic Monthly Press, 1990. $22.94. Informal account by ABC correspondent of travels through part of former Ottoman Empire ends with account of his capture as a hostage in Lebanon and his escape.

Kimball, Charles. *Religion, Politics and Oil: The Volatile Mix in the Middle East.* Nashville: Abingdon Press, 1991. $4.95, paper. Following an assessment of the U.S. churches reactions to the Gulf crisis and an overview of Islam, the dominant religious community in this region, explores major religious, politcal and economic factors influencing the Middle East following the 1991 Gulf war.

Lamb, David. *The Arabs—Journeys Beyond the Mirage.* New York: Random House, 1988. $9.95, paper. Exciting and sometimes disturbing sojourns throughout the Arab world. A useful, accessible survey of territories from Morocco to the Sudan, the West Bank to Saudi Arabia.

Salzman, Marian and O'Reilly, Ann. *War and Peace in the Persian Gulf: What Teenagers Want To Know.* Princeton, NJ: Peterson's Guides, 1991. $5.95. Written for teens, this straightforward book addresses everyone's concerns about the region in question and answer form. Typical question: "What kind of wildlife live in the Gulf Region and how were they affected by the war?"

Shabbas, Audrey, and Ayad Al-Qazzaz. *Arab World Notebook,* Secondary School Level, Berkeley, CA: Najda: Women Concerned About the Middle East. 1989, $39.95. An invaluable looseleaf notebook (including original material, reprints from magazines, classroom suggestions, and extensive bibliographies and filmographies) for anyone wanting to learn about Middle Eastern culture. Part I contains materials about 20 subject areas; Part II contains maps and data covering 21 countries.

Particular Areas and Nations

Abou-Saif, Laila. *Middle East Journal: A Woman's Journey into the Heart of the Arab World.* New York: Charles Scribners, 1990. $22.95 An Egyptian author's "attempt to bridge the gap between the Middle East and the West...," this book focuses on Egypt, and includes interviews with the nation's leaders to help Westerners "gain a deeper understanding of the Arab-Israeli dilemma."

Collins, Larry and Lapierre, Dominique. *O Jerusalem!* New York: Touchstone, Simon and Schuster, 1988. $10.95. Vividly recounts the struggle between Arabs and Jews in 1948 for Jerusalem. Presents both sides through stories of individuals and descriptions of meetings where high level decisions were made. Provides a backdrop for current situations.

Fisk, Robert. *Pity the Nation.* New York: Atheneum, 1990. $24.95. Written by one of the last remaining British correspondents for a major news organization based in Beirut, this book chronicles the tragedies of a country in the grips of chaos. Lengthy, detailed but readable.

Grossman, David. *The Yellow Wind,* Trans. from Hebrew by Haim Watzman. New York: Delacorte Books, 1988. $8.95. This impassioned, unusual account documents the observations of its acclaimed Israeli author during his three months of military service in the West Bank. One of the most controversial and fastest-selling books in the history of Israel.

Hiro, Dilip. *Iran Under the Ayatollahs.* London: Routledge Chapman & Hall, 1985. $17.95. This readable and informative book traces the development of Islam and the nation of Iran over the last 500 years. The book's three parts address the rise of the Islamic state; the overthrow of the monarchy and founding of the republic under Ayatollah Khomeini; and Iran's relations with the outside world.

al-Khalil, Samir. *Republic of Fear: The Inside Story of Saddam's Iraq.* New York: Pantheon, 1991. $12.95, paper. Superb account of how Saddaam Hussein and the Baath party took an entire society apart and put it back together, often using terror. By an Iraqi expatriate historian.

Kunstel, Marcia and Albright, Joseph. *Their Promised Land: Arab and Jews in Historys Cauldron.* New York: Crown Publishers, 1990. $19.95, paper. Two American journalists offer a well researched portrait of the Jews and Arabs who have lived in the Valley of Sorek, the home of the biblical hero Samson.

Mackey, Sandra. *The Saudis: Inside the Desert Kingdom.* New York: Signet, 1990. $5.95, paper. A rare firsthand glimpse by a U.S. woman into Saudi social and public life, where much remains hidden to outsiders.

Miller, Judith and Mylroie, Laurie. *Saddam Hussein and the Crisis in the Gulf.* New York: Times Books/Random House, 1991. $5.95, paper. Brisk, authoritative account of the "guns of August 1990," events that led up to Hussein's heist of Kuwait and Iraq's bid for primacy in the Middle East.

Mottahedeh, Roy. *The Mantle of the Prophet: Religion and Politics in Iran.* New York: Pantheon, 1991. $14.95, paper. Gifted historian weaves Iran's history around the life of a young mullah. Thoughtful look at the tensions between Persian culture and extremist religion.

Peretz, Don. *Intifada: The Palestinian Uprising.* Boulder, CO: Westview Press, 1990. $14.95. An excellent multi-dimensional study of the uprising that began in December 1987, in terms of political economic and social institutions of the Israelis and Palestinians, as well as the role of the United States.

Robins, Philip. *Turkey and the Middle East.* New York: Council of Foreign Relations Press, 1991. $14.95. A scholarly approach to Turkey, a Middle Eastern country often ignored. Turkey's politics are investigated as "a bundle of linkages," concerning Arab-Israeli politics as well as water and other domestic concerns.

Schiff, Ze'ev and Ya'ari, Ehud. Ed. and translated by Ina Friedman. *Intifada: The Palestinian Uprisings—Israel's Third Front.* New York: Simon & Schuster, 1990. $22.95. The Palestinian Uprising from an Israeli perspective: its roots and implications.

Seale, Patrick. *Asad: The Struggle for the Middle East.* Berkeley, CA: University of California Press, 1989. $25.00. A leading British journalist's "attempt to explain what the world looks like from the seat of power in Damascus." This sizeable effort contains much information on recent Middle Eastern history—such as the Syrian intervention into Lebanon, the 1973 War, Syria's role during the Iran-Iraq war.

Wright, Robin. *In the Name of God: The Khomeini Decade.* New York: Simon & Schuster, 1989. $19.95. Excellent account of Khomeini's Iran; provides overview and analysis of the stages of Iran's revolution.

Religion

Ellis, Marc H. *Toward a Jewish Theology of Liberation.* Maryknoll, New York: Orbis Books, 1987. $9.95, paper. The author, a Jewish theologian, shows the common roots of Judaism and Christianity in the Hebrew scripture, in order to make the argument that the liberation struggle is always two-sided.

al-Faruqi, Isma'il and Lamya, Lois. *The Cultural Atlas of Islam.* New York and London: Macmillan, 1986. $115. A marvelous comprehensive work that explains Islam—its beliefs, institutions, traditions and influences—in the context of the cultures in which the faith has taken root.

Johnson, Paul. *A History of the Jews.* New York: Harper Collins, 1988. $11.95, paper. Surveys 4000 years of the Jewish people through sections on Israelites, Judaism, Cathedocracy, Ghetto, Emancipation and Holocaust. [Pages 423-446 and 519-583 dealing with the development of Zionism are particularly useful.]

Ruether, Rosemary Radford and Ruether, Hermann J. *The Wrath of Jonah: The Crisis of Religious Nationalism in the Israeli-Palestinian Conflict.* San Francisco: Harper & Row, 1989. $19.95. Deep concern for understanding this conflict in terms of its history, religious connections, ethical values and need for reconciliation. The aim is to bring forward ethical norms that Christians, Jews and Muslims can recognize and affirm.

Christianity

Cragg, Kenneth. *Arab Christians.* Louisville: Westminster/John Knox Press, 1991. $29.95. The most thorough, up-to-date study (in English) of the history of Christianity in the Arab-speaking Middle East. Not easy reading, but those who work their way through will be rewarded.

Colbi, Saul P. *A History of the Christian Presence in the Holy Land.* Lanham, MD: University Press of America, 1988. $28.50. A wealth of information about institutional Christianity in the region from the beginning to 1986. Includes background on conflicts over the holy places and the populations of various Christian denomination.

Ateek, Naim Stifan. *Justice and Only Justice: A Palestinian Theology of Liberation.* Maryknoll, NY: Orbis Books, 1989. $12.95. Writing as a Palestinian, a Christian, an Arab and as a citizen of the State of Israel, the author (Canon of St. George's Cathedral in Jerusalem), focuses on the biblical concept of justice in order to provide a Christian theological lens through which to view the situation.

Magazines. Articles on The Middle East from a Christian perspective are often featured in *The Christian Century, Christianity and Crisis,* and *Sojourners.* Recommended also is the Fall 1991 *Media & Values,* an issue on "The Media:

In War and Peace," which examines in depth the way the Gulf war and its participants were portrayed (or ignored). Single issue $4 from Center for Media and Values, 1962 Shenandoah, Los Angeles, CA 90034.

Culture, Including Women and Family Life

Corey, Helen. *Food from Biblical Lands*, available from Americans for Middle East Understanding. $16.95. Two special features of this cookbook are the how-to photographs and the sections on Lenten and other traditional Christian foods from Syria.

El Saadawi, Nawal. *The Hidden Face of Eve: Women in the Arab World*, Boston: Beacon Press, 1982. $9.95, paper. In a fearless book, Egypt's former Director of Public Health describes the problems of growing up female in the Islamic world. The author believes that the oppression of women derives from the class and patriarchal system rather than any specific religion or culture.

Fernea, Elizabeth Warnock, and Berzigan, Basima Qattan. *Middle Eastern Muslim Women Speak*. Austin, TX: University of Texas Press, 1977. $11.50. Women from a variety of historical periods are given voice through their own writings and the words of others in this extensive anthology. Includes sections from the Qur'an relating to women and a healthy sprinkling of poetry.

Gadant, Monique, ed. *Women of the Mediterranean*. London: Zed Press, 1986. Distributed by Humanities Press: Atlantic Highlands, NJ. $12.50. Articles and first person stories by 19 women, (including an Algerian midwife, a Turkish social worker and an official of the Union of Palestinian Women). Stories center around common themes.

Nydell, Margaret K. *Understanding Arabs: A Guide for Westerners*. Yarmouth ME: Intercultural Press, Inc., 1987. $15.95. A cross-cultural handbook provides information about Arab values and social practices for non-Arabs. Helps to dispel stereotypes and opens the reader to new ways of viewing the Arab world.

Roden, Claudia. *A New Book of Middle Eastern Food*, New York: Viking Penquin, 1985. New, enlarged edition of book listed in food section, with more than 500 recipes plus an extensive commentary on cooking, eating customs, and food traditions. The 1974 edition men tioned elsewhere in the guide (New York: Knopf, 1974) is $13.95.

Shaabane, Bouthaina. *Both Right and Left Handed: Arab Women Talk About Their Lives*, Bloomington, IN: Indiana University Press, 1988. $12.95. Breaking the stereotype of the passive Arab woman, this newly reprinted book contains interviews with bright, assertive women and a glimpse into their world and struggles.

Literature

Bushnaq, Inea, translator and editor. *Arab Folktales*, New York: Pantheon Books, 1986, $11.95. Stories of the wise and not-so-wise, of animals and bedouins, of morality and of the supernatural, drawn from previous collections as well as the author's own tapes and experiences.

Mahfouz, Naguib. *Palace Walk*. Translated by William M. Hutchings and Olive E. Kenny. New York: Anchor-Doubleday, 1990. Paper, $9.95. The first novel of a trilogy now being translated into English, by the Nobel prize winning Egyptian author. An early 20th-century Egyptian merchant struggles to use the teachings of Islam to protect his family from a world he finds difficult to understand. The author's style has been compared to Balzac and Dickens.

Muhawi, Ibrahim and Kanaana, Sharif. *Speak, Bird, Speak Again: Palestinian Arab Folktales*. Berkeley: University of California Press, 1988. $15.95, paper. A collection of charming—and often pungent—folktales with detailed glosses that shed light on aspects of popular Arab culture.

Rifaat, Alifa. *Distant View of a Minaret and Other Stories*. Translated by Denys Johnson Davies. New York: Quartet Books, 1983. Short stories by an Eqyptian Muslim woman provide a unique perspective on urban and rural life in modern Egypt.

Children

Alexander, Sue. *Nadia, the Willful*. New York: Pantheon, 1983. $12.95. Oasis dweller Nadia changes her father's approach to death.

Ashabranner, Brent. *Gavriel and Jemal, Two Boys of Jerusalem*, New York, NY: Putnam Publishing Group, 1984, $11.95. Photo essay of the everyday life of a Muslim and an Orthodox Jewish boy living near each other in the Old City.

Cohen, Barbara. *Seven Daughters and Seven Sons*. New York: Athenaeum, 1984. out of print but available in libraries. A book-length retelling of an Iraqi folktale.

Haskins, Jim. *Count Your Way Through the Arab World*. Minneapolis: Carolrhoda Books, 1987. $4.95, paper. Arab village life unfolds by counting in Arabic from one to ten. Grades 2-4.

Schami, Rafik. *A Hand Full of Stars*. New York: Dutton Children's Books, 1987 (1990). $14.95. Internationally acclaimed diary of a Syrian boy's efforts to become a journalist after family poverty forced him to drop out of school in Damascus. For teenagers.

Stickles, Frances. *The Flag Balloon*. Washington, DC: American Educational Trust, 1988. The heroine defies the soldiers to make and fly a flag over her town in the Occupied Territories. Grades 2-6.

Soghikian, Juanita Will. *Lands, Peoples and Communities of the Middle East*. Fountain Hills, AZ: Middle East Gateway Series (See page 26 for address). Resources including a text, teacher's guide, wall map, game kit and a booklet of duplicating masters. Grades 3-6.

☆

Filmography

PRIMARY RESOURCES

CELEBRATION OF LIFE
1/2" VHS   Sale: S39.95   28:30 minutes
                  Rental: $20.00

A sense of life in the Middle East, as influenced by the religions of the area, is powerfully depicted here as people live out their faith and daily life despite conflicts, violations of human rights, and constant power struggles. The role of the Christian church is honestly portrayed—from the Crusades and early missionaries to current efforts of the Middle East Council of Churches to promote unity, service, and witness. Gabriel Habib, Executive for the MECC, speaks about the Council's present role amidst the conflict. The video ends with a Palm Sunday procession leading to new hope in the resurrected Christ. A video to help you experience life in the Middle East today.

Available for sale only ($39.95) from:
  Friendship Press Distribution Office
  P.O. Box 37844
  Cincinnati, OH 45222-0844
  513-948-8733
Available for rental only ($20.00) from:
  EcuFilm (see below)

AFTER THE STORM: POWER AND PEACE IN THE MIDDLE EAST
1/2" VHS   Sale: $19.95   28:00 minutes

Recent events in the Middle East now make it more important than ever for North American church members who are concerned about peace and justice to learn as much as possible about the people and the countries of this region. "After the Storm" presents a quick, helpful overview and introduction to the Middle East's history, geography, cultures, languages, religion, economics, and politics. Through stills and narration, viewers are given information which will help them as they work through this study. Ecumenical in perspective, this video is designed to stimulate congregational study and discussion. Study guide included.

Available for sale onlv ($19.95) from:
  Friendship Press Distribution Office (see above).

SECONDARY RESOURCES

BEHIND THE FLAG: COSTS OF THE GULF WAR
1/2" VHS   sale: $22.00   20:00 minutes

This emotionally powerful video looks at the many costs ot the Gulf War: costs to Iraq, to the Third World, to the environment, and finally to the U.S. in terms of quallty of life and status in the world. Also, the performance of U.S. media in reporting the war is addressed. The video contains footage from wartime Iraq and commentary from a retired admiral, a former ambassador to Saudi Arabia, and the president of the Southern Christian Leadership Conference, among others. Deals with complex issues in a helpful way. **Study guide** included.

From: Educational Media Associates (see below)

FAMILY TIES
1/2" VHS   Sale: $250.00   50:00 minutes
                  Rental: $50.00

This video centers around the mother of a large extended family of Jordanians living in Amman. We meet women who have different views of the traditional role of wives and mothers, a Tunisian girl who longs to find her own apartment, and a Jordanian woman who is a commercial pilot flying jets. [NOTE: from a series of ten 50-minute documentaries called "The Arabs: A Living history," which explores Arab history, culture and society through the lives and opinions of Arabs today. Write Landmark for a complete listing of this series.]

From: Landmark Films, Inc. (see below)

THE FORGOTTEN FAITHFUL
1/2" VHS   Sale: $29.95   30:00 minutes

A look at the Palestinian Christians, who are bringing up children as Christians while living under occupation. This indigenous church has been in the Holy Land for centuries, yet is often forgotten by North American Christians. Tourists visit sacred sites and miss these "living stones," the community of the Christian faith that has existed on these lands from the very beginning.

From: EcuFilm (see below)

GIANT OF THE GULF
1/2" VHS   Sale: $250.00   42:00 minutes
                  Rental: $50.00

Iran is destined to emerge as one of the most important powers in the Gulf region. This video documents how Iran is transforming itself from the bastion of Islamic fundamentalism into an economic, political, and military superpower. After the Iran-Iraq war a more pragmatic leadership has risen in Iran which is helping it to fulfill its vast economic potential. The video also looks at the reactions to these developments from Islamic fundamentalists.

PROM: Landmark Pilms, Inc. (see below)

HOPE FOR LIFE
1/2" VHS   Sale: $34.95   36:00 minutes
16mm film   Rental: $15.00

Filmed in Egypt, Lebanon, the West Bank, and Gaza, this documentary looks at the many ministries of Christian mission and service in the Middle East. The various scenes and people in the film are bound together by spiritual elements such as the events of Holy Week, an Orthodox communion service, and the ceremony of the Holy Fire in Old Jerusalem. Though filmed in 1978 and thus somewhat dated, it conveys a sense of the Christian presence in the Middle East.

From: EcuFilm (see below)

JORDAN'S STORMY BANKS: 1991
1/2" VHS   Sale: $19.95   25:00 minutes

Three major faith groups trace their roots back to Abraham: Judaism, Christianity, and Islam. The relations between the three have a long and sometimes troubled history as outlined in this timely video (a 1991 re-make of an earlier filmstrip). It focuses on the present conflicts between the Palestinians (mostly Muslim, mostly Arab) and Israelis (mostly Jews). This video draws on the perspectives of Christian denominations and ecumenical bodies for its interpretations. It will help viewers better understand the Israeli-Palestinian conflict. Leader's Guide.

From: EcuFilm (see below)

KURDISTAN—THE LAST COLONY?
1/2" VHS   Sale: $250.00   52:00 minutes
              Rental: $50.00

Inside Kurdistan the Kurds languish under the imposition of alien languages, cultures, and political orders. Beyond its borders, hundreds of thousands of Kurds live in exile. This video explores the phenomenon of a nation of more than 25 million condemned to stand divided by frontiers forged within living memory. It traces Kurdish history from pre-Babylonian times to the present, examines the Kurdish national movement in those nations which now control their lands, and shows attacks mounted on the civilian population by Iraqi and Iranian forces and the widespread Kurdish resistance.

From: Landmark Films, Inc. (see below)

LINES IN THE SAND
1/2" VHS   Sale: $21.95   10:00 minutes

Featuring footage shot in Iraq by one of the first groups of Americans to enter Baghdad after the war, this video essay raises some questions that the media forgot during Operation Desert Storm. In a thought-provoking style, it traces the evolution of military press and information-control strategies from Vietnam through Central America in the 1980s and to the Persian Gulf War. It looks at the human cost of the war and examines the threat posed to democracy by an unchecked national security state.

From: Griffin-Wirth Associates (see below)

THE PRICE OF CHANGE
1/2" VHS   Rental: $20.00   26:00 minutes

For 60 years Egyptian women gradually have been entering their nation's labor force. Work outside the home, once considered shameful, has become necessary. This film examines the consequences of working on five women, including a factory worker, a doctor, and an opposition member of Egypt's Parliament. It presents a picture of changing attitudes toward work, family, sex, and the woman's place in society. Produced in 1982.

FROM: EcuFilm (see below)

RIVERS OF FIRE
1/2" VHS   Free Loan   40:00 minutes

Highlights a little-knows Middle East conflict over a natural resource more valuable than oil—*water*. The interrelationship between basic need versus limited supplies and heightened use, along with inflammatory political overtones, equal a volatile situation. Control of water is the ultimate weapor the Middle East; it will continue to threaten stability in a region where increasing populations demand more water. Human and environmental catastrophe could result before the end of the century.

From: Church World Service Film Library (see below)

THE SHADOW OF THE WEST
1/2" VHS   Sale: $250.00   50:00 minutes
              Rental: $50.00

Focus here is on the plight of the Palestinians, which can be seen as an enduring residue of the modern encounter between the Arabs and the West. Edward Said traces the course of European involvement with the Near East via the Crusades to Napoleon's campaign in Egypt and the French and English entrepreneurs, adventurers, and empire builders who came in his wake. From a series of ten 50-minute documentaries called "The Arabs: A Living History." Write Landmark for a complete listing.

From: Landmark Films, Inc. (see below)

TALKING TO THE ENEMY: VOICES OF SORROW AND RAGE
1/2" VHS   Sale: $445.00   54:00 minutes
              Rental: $75.00

Amid the seething conflict between Israel and Palestine, a young Palestinian journalist and an older Israeli editor try to negotiate their own peace. Chaim Shur invited Muna Hamzeh to visit his kibbutz. Muna's arrival unleashes a passionate dialogue as old wounds are reopened. The reconciliation they had hoped to accomplish was not to be. But out of this meeting comes a mutual compassion for the pain each has suffered. 1988.

From: Filmakers Library (see below)

DISTRIBUTORS

Church World Service Film Library
P.O. Box 968
28606 Phillips Street
Elkhart, IN 46515
219-264-3102

EcuFilm
810 Twelfth Avenue, South
Nashville, TN 37203
800-251-4091

Educational Media Associates
5311 Western Avenue
Boulder, CO 80303
303-442-6055

Filmaker's Library
124 E. 40th Street
New York, NY 10016
212-808-4980

Griffin-Wirth Associates
168 Parkway Drive
Syracuse, NY 13207
315-471-4953

Landmark Films, Inc.
3450 Slade Run Drive
Falls Church, VA 22042
800-342-4336 703-241-2030

Morehouse Publishing
3000 Canby Street
Harrisburg, PA 17103
800-272-5484

These previously published books from Friendship Press are mentioned in this guide and will be useful additional resources for your study. The information for ordering these books is on the inside back cover this guide.

GOD IS ONE: The Way of Islam

Marston Speight

Written by a committed Christians and former missionary, this book offers a sensitive presentation of the faith that unites one-fifth of the world's people. It answers basic questions of who Muslims are and what they believe, and discusses the common ground for Muslim-Christian dialogue. Illustrated with examples of Islam's contributions to science, art, literature.
ISBN 0-377-00196-1 $5.95

ONE GOD, TWO FAITHS: When Christians and Muslims Meet
Study Guide on the World of Islam

Sarah Klos

A six-session study guide that helps groups explore Islam's history and beliefs. Joining in dramas and conversations encourages them to get to know Muslims as neighbors and grow in their own Christian faith. Includes such extra activities as visiting a mosque.
ISBN 0-377-00197-X $4.95

NEIGHBORS: Muslims in North America

Interviews by Elias Mallon

Muslims in communities across North America talk freely about their families, work, and spiritual journeys in a faith that many of their neighbors regard with suspicion. These interviews shatter stereotypes as real men and women say who they are and what they believe.
ISBN 0-377-00198-8 $5.95

UNIFIED IN HOPE: Arabs and Jews Talk About Peace

Interviews by Carol J. Birkland

Honest and deeply moving, these stories by and about nineteen real Palestinians and Israelis challenge attitudes that have long resisted change .
ISBN 0-377-00177-5 $8.95

EYES TO SEE, EARS TO HEAR
Study Guide to "Peoples and Churches of the USSR"

Betty Jane Bailey and Constance J. Tarasar

The explanations, activities and resources focusing on worship in the Orthodox tradition will be helpful in understanding Orthodox churches in the Middle East (icons, the church calendar, the role of women, liturgy, spirituality, a plan for visiting an Orthodox church).
ISBN 0-377-00168-6 $5.95